XML and XSL

XML and XSL

Preeti Jain

CENTRUM PRESS
NEW DELHI-110002 (INDIA)

CENTRUM PRESS
H.O.: 4360/4, Ansari Road, Daryaganj,
New Delhi-110002 (India)
Tel: 23278000, 23261597, 23255577, 23286875
B.O.: No. 1015, Ist Main Road, BSK IIIrd Stage,
IIIrd Phase, IIIrd Block, Bangalore-560085 (INDIA)
Tel: 080-41723429
Email: centrumpress@gmail.com
Visit us at: www.centrumpress.com

XML and XSL

First Edition, 2011

PRINTED IN INDIA

Printed at Tarun Offset Printers, Delhi-110053

Contents

Preface

XSL is a scripting language that can be used to generate HTML from data in XML form. The Collectorz.com programs use XSL templates to show, export and print items. To do this, the programs first create temporary XML documents containing the data for the selected item(s), then use XSL scripts to generate the HTML page(s). When the program starts it scans the Templates subfolder for available *.CTI files (Collectorz.com Template Info files). These CTI files contain information about the templates (description, template type, item type, etc.). After that the templates show up in the appropriate template selection lists in the program, depending on the template and item types defined in the CTI files. See below for more info about the CTI file format. The XML format used by the Collectorz.com programs consists of two sections, the meta data and the collection data.

The metadata part contains information about the field names used in the program. This information can be used to make your template show the user's own field names automatically. Take a look at the included templates to see how this is done.

Author

1

HTML/XML

INTRODUCTION

HTML

HTML is a subset of SGML, the most frequently used document type in the Web. It defines a single, fixed type of document with markup that lets you describe a common class of simple office style report, with headings, paragraphs, lists, illustrations, etc., and some provision for hypertext and multimedia.

HTML was defined to allow the transfer, display and linking of documents over the internet and is the key enabling technology for the WWW. Prior to the emerging of the internet, it was unusual in the word of computing to hear the word "page" used to describe elements of data. But HTML web pages have amazing similarities with paper in their role of information publishing.

Both HTML and paper pages:

- Are optimized for visual clarity,
- Focus on ultimate usability (but not on reusability),
- Contain no contextual information, and
- Have no document structure to enable automation.

Today's web is created by Hand for Eyes only. HTML has too low an "Information IQ" to +enable many desirable applications. HTML was designed as a markup language an with simple structures, strong emphasis on formatting and was weak for encoding content. It was not designed to encode structure and semantics needed for complex applications.

WHAT IS HTML

To publish information for global distribution, one needs a universally understood language, a kind of publishing mother tongue that all computers may potentially understand. The publishing language used by the World Wide Web is HTML (from HyperText Markup Language).

HTML gives authors the means to:

- Publish online documents with headings, text, tables, lists, photos, etc.
- Retrieve online information via hypertext links, at the click of a button.
- Design forms for conducting transactions with remote services, for use in searching for information, making reservations, ordering products, etc.
- Include spread-sheets, video clips, sound clips, and other applications directly in their documents.

A BRIEF HISTORY OF HTML

HTML was originally developed by Tim Berners-Lee while at CERN, and popularized by the Mosaic browser developed at NCSA. During the course of the 1990s it has blossomed with the explosive growth of the Web. During this time, HTML has been extended in a number of ways. The Web depends on Web page authors and vendors sharing the same conventions for HTML. This has motivated joint work on specifications for HTML.

HTML 2.0 (November 1995, see [RFC1866]) was developed under the aegis of the Internet Engineering Task Force (IETF) to codify common practice in late 1994. HTML+ (1993) and HTML 3.0 (1995, see [HTML30]) proposed much richer versions of HTML. Despite never receiving consensus in standards discussions, these drafts led to the adoption of a range of new features. The efforts of the World Wide Web Consortium's HTML Working Group to codify common practice in 1996 resulted in HTML 3.2 (January 1997, [HTML32]). Changes from HTML 3.2 are summarized in Appendix A Most people agree that HTML documents should work well across different browsers and platforms. Achieving interoperability lowers costs to content providers since they must develop only one version of a document. If the effort is not made, there is much greater risk that the Web will devolve into a proprietary world of incompatible formats, ultimately reducing the Web's commercial potential for all participants.

Each version of HTML has attempted to reflect greater consensus among industry players so that the investment made by content providers will not be wasted and that their documents will not become unreadable in a short period of time.

HTML has been developed with the vision that all manner of devices should be able to use information on the Web: PCs with graphics displays of varying resolution and colour depths, cellular telephones, hand held devices, devices for speech for output and input, computers with high or low bandwidth, and so on.

HTML 4.0

HTML 4.0 extends HTML with mechanisms for style sheets, scripting, frames, embedding objects, improved support for right to left and mixed direction text, richer tables, and enhancements to forms, offering improved accessibility for people with disabilities.

Internationalization

This version of HTML has been designed with the help of experts in the field of internationalization, so that documents may be written in every language and be transported easily around the world. This has been accomplished by incorporating [RFC2070], which deals with the internationalization of HTML.

One important step has been the adoption of the ISO/ IEC:10646 standard ([ISO10646]) as the document character set for HTML. This is the world's most inclusive standard dealing with issues of the representation of international characters, text direction, punctuation, and other world language issues.

HTML now offers greater support for diverse human languages within a document. This allows for more effective indexing of documents for search engines, higher-quality typography, better text-to-speech conversion, better hyphenation, etc.

Accessibility

As the Web community grows and its members diversify in their abilities and skills, it is crucial that the underlying technologies be appropriate to their specific needs. HTML has been designed to make Web pages more accessible to those with physical limitations.

HTML 4.0 developments inspired by concerns for accessibility include:

- Better distinction between document structure and presentation, thus encouraging the use of style sheets instead of HTML presentation elements and attributes.
- Better forms, including the addition of access keys, the ability to group form controls semantically, the ability to group select options semantically, and active labels.
- The ability to markup a text description of an included object (with the object element).
- A new client-side image map mechanism (the MAP element) that allows authors to integrate image and text links.
- The requirement that alternate text accompany images included with the IMG element and image maps included with the AREA element.
- Support for the title and lang attributes on all elements.
- Support for the ABBR and Acronym elements.
- A wider range of target media (tty, braille, etc.) for use with style sheets.
- Better tables, including captions, column groups, and mechanisms to facilitate non-visual rendering.
- Long descriptions of tables, images, frames, etc.

Authors who design pages with accessibility issues in mind will not only receive the blessings of the accessibility community, but will benefit in other ways as well: well-designed HTML documents that distinguish structure and presentation will adapt more easily to new technologies.

Note. For more information about designing accessible HTML documents, please consult [WAIGUIDE].

Tables

The new table model in HTML is based on [RFC1942]. Authors now have greater control over structure and layout (*e.g.*, column groups). The ability of designers to recommend column widths allows user agents to display table data incrementally (as it arrives) rather than waiting for the entire table before rendering.

Note. At the time of writing, some HTML authoring tools rely extensively on tables for formatting, which may easily cause accessibility problems.

Compound Documents

HTML now offers a standard mechanism for embedding generic media objects and applications in HTML documents. The OBJECT element (together with its more specific ancestor elements IMG and APPLET) provides a mechanism for including images, video, sound, mathematics, specialized applications, and other objects in a document. It also allows authors to specify a hierarchy of alternate renderings for user agents that don't support a specific rendering.

Style Sheets

Style sheets simplify HTML markup and largely relieve HTML of the responsibilities of presentation. They give both authors and users control over the presentation of documents — font information, alignment, colours, etc.

Style information can be specified for individual elements or groups of elements. Style information may be specified in an HTML document or in external style sheets.

The mechanisms for associating a style sheet with a document is independent of the style sheet language. Before the advent of style sheets, authors had limited control over rendering. HTML 3.2 included a number of attributes and elements offering control over alignment, font size, and text colour. Authors also exploited tables and images as a means for laying out pages.

The relatively long time it takes for users to upgrade their browsers means that these features will continue to be used for some time. However, since style sheets offer more powerful presentation mechanisms, the World Wide Web Consortium will eventually phase out many of HTML's presentation elements and attributes. Throughout the specification elements and attributes at risk are marked as "deprecated". They are accompanied by examples of how to achieve the same effects with other elements or style sheets.

Scripting

Through scripts, authors may create dynamic Web pages (*e.g.*, "smart forms" that react as users fill them out) and use HTML as a means to build networked applications. The mechanisms provided to include scripts in an HTML document are independent of the scripting language.

Printing

Sometimes, authors will want to make it easy for users to print more than just the current document. When documents form part of a larger work, the relationships between them can be described using the HTML LINK element or using W3C's Resource Description Language (RDF) (see [RDF]).

AUTHORING DOCUMENTS WITH HTML 4.0

We recommend that authors and implementors observe the following general principles when working with HTML 4.0.

Separate Structure and Presentation

HTML has its roots in SGML which has always been a language for the specification of structural markup. As HTML matures, more and more of its presentational elements and attributes are being replaced by other mechanisms, in particular style sheets. Experience has shown that separating the structure of a document from its presentational aspects reduces the cost of serving a wide range of platforms, media, etc., and facilitates document revisions.

Consider Universal Accessibility to the Web

To make the Web more accessible to everyone, notably those with disabilities, authors should consider how their documents may be rendered on a variety of platforms: speech-based browsers, braille-readers, etc. We do not recommend that authors limit their creativity, only that they consider alternate renderings in their design. HTML offers a number of mechanisms to this end (*e.g.*, the alt attribute, the accesskey attribute, etc.)

Furthermore, authors should keep in mind that their documents may be reaching a far-off audience with different computer configurations. In order for documents to be interpreted correctly, authors should include in their documents information about the natural language and direction of the text, how the document is encoded, and other issues related to internationalization.

HELP USER AGENTS WITH INCREMENTAL RENDERING

By carefully designing their tables and making use of new table features in HTML 4.0, authors can help user agents render documents more quickly. Authors can learn how to design tables for incremental rendering (see the TABLE element). Implementors should consult the notes on tables in the appendix for information on incremental algorithms.

WHAT IS THE WORLD WIDE WE

The *World Wide Web (Web)* is a network of information resources.

The Web relies on three mechanisms to make these resources readily available to the widest possible audience:

1. A uniform naming scheme for locating resources on the Web (*e.g.*, URIs).

2. Protocols, for access to named resources over the Web (*e.g.*, HTTP).
3. Hypertext, for easy navigation among resources (*e.g.*, HTML).

The ties between the three mechanisms are apparent throughout this specification.

INTRODUCTION TO URIS

Every resource available on the Web — HTML document, image, video clip, programme, etc. — has an address that may be encoded by a *Universal Resource Identifier*, or "URI".

URIs typically consist of three pieces:

1. The naming scheme of the mechanism used to access the resource.
2. The name of the machine hosting the resource.
3. The name of the resource itself, given as a path.

Consider the URI that designates the current HTML specification:

This URI may be read as follows: There is a document available via the HTTP protocol (see [RFC2068]), residing on the machine www.w3.org, accessible via the path "/TR/REC-html4/". Other schemes you may see in HTML documents include "mailto" for e-mail and "ftp" for FTP.

Here is another example of a URI. This one refers to a user's mailbox:

```
...this is text...
For all comments, please send e-mail to
<A href="mailto:joe@someplace.com">Joe Cool</A>.
```

Note. Most readers may be familiar with the term "URL" and not the term "URI". URLs form a subset of the more general URI naming scheme.

FRAGMENT IDENTIFIERS

Some URIs refer to a location within a resource. This kind of URI ends with "#" followed by an anchor identifier (called the *fragment identifier*). For instance, here is a URI pointing to an anchor named section_2:

```
http://somesite.com/html/top.html#section_2
```

RELATIVE URIS

A *relative URI* doesn't contain any naming scheme information. Its path generally refers to a resource on the same machine as the current document. Relative URIs may contain relative path components (*e.g.*, ".." means one level up in the hierarchy defined by the path), and may contain fragment identifiers. Relative URIs are resolved to full URIs using a base URI. As an example of relative URI resolution, assume we have the base URI "http://www.acme.com/support/intro.html". The relative URI in the following markup for a hypertext link:

```
<A href="suppliers.html">Suppliers</A>
```

would expand to the full URI "http://www.acme.com/support/suppliers.html", while the relative URI in the following markup for an image

```
<IMG src="../icons/logo.gif" alt="logo">
```

would expand to the full URI "http://www.acme.com/icons/logo.gif".

In HTML, URIs are used to:

- Link to another document or resource, (the A and LINK elements).
- Link to an external style sheet or script (see the LINK and SCRIPT elements).
- Include an image, object, or applets in a page, (see the IMG, OBJECT, APPLET and INPUT elements).
- Create an image map (the MAP and AREA elements).
- Submit a form (FORM).
- Create a frame document (the FRAME and IFRAME elements).
- Cite an external reference The Q, BLOCKQUOTE, INS and DEL elements).
- Refer to metadata conventions describing a document (see the HEAD element).

Please consult the section on the URI type for more information about URIs.

ABOUT HTML

To publish information for global distribution, one needs a universally understood language, a kind of publishing mother tongue that all computers may potentially understand. The publishing language used by the World Wide Web is HTML (from HyperText Markup Language).

HTML gives authors the means to:

- Publish online documents with headings, text, tables, lists, photos, etc.
- Retrieve online information via hypertext links, at the click of a button.
- Design forms for conducting transactions with remote services, for use in searching for information, making reservations, ordering products, etc.
- Include spread-sheets, video clips, sound clips, and other applications directly in their documents.

A BRIEF HISTORY OF HTML

HTML was originally developed by Tim Berners-Lee while at CERN, and popularized by the Mosaic browser developed at NCSA. During the course of the 1990s it has blossomed with the explosive growth of the Web. During this time, HTML has been extended in a number of ways. The Web depends on Web page authors and vendors sharing the same conventions for HTML. This has motivated joint work on specifications for HTML.

HTML 2.0 (November 1995, see [RFC1866]) was developed under the aegis of the Internet Engineering Task Force (IETF) to codify common practice in late 1994. HTML+ (1993) and HTML 3.0 (1995, [HTML30]) proposed much richer versions of HTML.

Despite never receiving consensus in standards discussions, these drafts led to the adoption of a range of new features. The efforts of the World Wide Web Consortium's HTML Working Group to codify common practice in 1996 resulted in HTML 3.2 (January 1997, [HTML32]). Changes from HTML 3.2 are summarized in Appendix A

Most people agree that HTML documents should work well across different browsers and platforms. Achieving interoperability lowers costs to content providers since they must develop only one version of a document. If the effort is not made, there is much greater risk that the Web will devolve into a proprietary world of incompatible formats, ultimately reducing the Web's commercial potential for all participants.

Each version of HTML has attempted to reflect greater consensus among industry players so that the investment made by content providers will not be wasted and that their documents will not become unreadable in a short period of time.

HTML has been developed with the vision that all manner of devices should be able to use information on the Web: PCs with graphics displays of varying resolution and colour depths, cellular telephones, hand held devices, devices for speech for output and input, computers with high or low bandwidth, and so on.

XML BASIC

WHAT IS XML

- XML stands for EXtensible Markup Language
- XML is a markup language much like HTML
- XML was designed to carry data, not to display data
- XML tags are not predefined. You must define your own tags
- XML is designed to be self-descriptive
- XML is a W3C Recommendation
- *XML:* eXtensible Markup Language

XML is a framework for defining markup languages:

- There is no fixed collection of markup tags–we may define our own tags, tailored for our kind of information
- Each XML language is targeted at its own application domain, but the languages will share many features
- there is a common set of generic tools for processing documents

XML is not a replacement for HTML:

- HTML should ideally be just another XML language
- In fact, XHTML is just that

- XHTML is a (very popular) XML language for hypertext markup

XML is designed to:

- Separate syntax from semantics to provide a common framework for structuring information (browser rendering semantics is completely defined by stylesheets);
- Allow tailor-made markup for any imaginable application domain
- Support internationalization (Unicode) and platform independence
- Be the future of structured information, including databases

The Difference Between XML and HTML

XML is not a replacement for HTML:

XML and HTML were designed with different goals:

- XML was designed to transport and store data, with focus on what data is.
- HTML was designed to display data, with focus on how data looks.

HTML is about displaying information, while XML is about carrying information.

XML Does not DO Anything

Maybe it is a little hard to understand, but XML does not DO anything. XML was created to structure, store, and transport information.

The following example is a note to Tove from Jani, stored as XML:

```
<note>
<to>Tove</to>
<from>Jani</from>
<heading>Reminder</heading>
<body>Don't forget me this weekend!</body>
</note>
```

The note above is quite self descriptive. It has sender and receiver information, it also has a heading and a message body.

But still, this XML document does not DO anything. It is just pure information wrapped in tags. Someone must write a piece of software to send, receive or display it.

XML is Just Plain Text

XML is nothing special. It is just plain text. Software that can handle plain text can also handle XML. However, XML-aware applications can handle the XML tags specially. The functional meaning of the tags depends on the nature of the application.

With XML You Invent Your Own Tags

The tags in the example above (like <to> and <from>) are not defined in any XML standard. These tags are "invented" by the author of the XML document.

That is because the XML language has no predefined tags.

The tags used in HTML (and the structure of HTML) are predefined. HTML documents can only use tags defined in the HTML standard (like <p>, <h1>, etc.). XML allows the author to define his own tags and his own document structure.

XML is Not a Replacement for HTML

XML is a complement to HTML: It is important to understand that XML is not a replacement for HTML. In most web applications, XML is used to transport data, while HTML is used to format and display the data.

My best description of XML is this: XML is a software- and hardware-independent tool for carrying information.

XML is a W3C Recommendation

XML became a W3C Recommendation 10. February 1998.

To read more about the XML activities at W3C, please read our W3C Tutorial.

XML is Everywhere

We have been participating in XML development since its creation. It has been amazing to see how quickly the XML standard has developed, and how quickly a large number of software vendors has adopted the standard. XML is now as important for the Web as HTML was to the foundation of the Web. XML is everywhere. It is the most common tool for data transmissions between all sorts of applications, and is becoming more and more popular in the area of storing and describing information.

XML HOW TO USE

XML is used in many aspects of web development, often to simplify data storage and sharing.

XML Separates Data from HTML

If you need to display dynamic data in your HTML document, it will take a lot of work to edit the HTML each time the data changes.

With XML, data can be stored in separate XML files. This way you can concentrate on using HTML for layout and display, and be sure that changes in the underlying data will not require any changes to the HTML.

With a few lines of JavaScript, you can read an external XML file and update the data content of your HTML. You will learn more about this.

XML Simplifies Data Sharing

In the real world, computer systems and databases contain data in incompatible formats. XML data is stored in plain text format. This provides a software- and hardware-independent way of storing data. This makes it much easier to create data that different applications can share.

XML Simplifies Data Transport

With XML, data can easily be exchanged between incompatible systems. One of the most time-consuming challenges for developers is to exchange data between incompatible systems over the Internet.

Exchanging data as XML greatly reduces this complexity, since the data can be read by different incompatible applications.

XML Simplifies Platform Changes

Upgrading to new systems (hardware or software platforms), is always very time consuming. Large amounts of data must be converted and incompatible data is often lost.

XML data is stored in text format. This makes it easier to expand or upgrade to new operating systems, new applications, or new browsers, without losing data.

XML Makes Your Data More Available

Since XML is independent of hardware, software and application, XML can make your data more available and useful. Different applications can access your data, not only in HTML pages, but also from XML data sources. With XML, your data can be available to all kinds of"reading machines" (Handheld computers, voice machines, news feeds, etc), and make it more available for blind people, or people with other disabilities.

XML is Used to Create New Internet Languages

A lot of new Internet languages are created with XML.
Here are some examples:

- XHTML the latest version of HTML
- WSDL for describing available web services
- WAP and WML as markup languages for handheld devices
- RSS languages for news feeds
- RDF and OWL for describing resources and ontology
- SMIL for describing multimedia for the web

If Developers Have Sense

If they DO have sense, future applications will exchange their data in XML. The future might give us word processors, spreadsheet applications and databases that can read each other's data in a pure text format, without any conversion utilities in between. We can only pray that all the software vendors will agree.

XML TREE

XML documents form a tree structure that starts at"the root" and branches to"the leaves".

An Example XML Document

XML documents use a self-describing and simple syntax:

```
<?xml version="1.0" encoding="ISO-8859-1"?>
<note>
  <to>Tove</to>
  <from>Jani</from>
  <heading>Reminder</heading>
  <body>Don't forget me this weekend!</body>
</note>
```

The first line is the XML declaration. It defines the XML version (1.0) and the encoding used (ISO-8859-1 = Latin-1/West European character set).

The next line describes the root element of the document (like saying:"this document is a note"):

```
<note>
```

The next 4 lines describe 4 child elements of the root (to, from, heading, and body):

```
<to>Tove</to>
<from>Jani</from>
<heading>Reminder</heading>
<body>Don't forget me this weekend!</body>
```

And finally the last line defines the end of the root element:

```
</note>
```

You can assume, from this example, that the XML document contains a note to Tove from Jani. Don't you agree that XML is pretty self-descriptive?

XML Documents Form a Tree Structure

XML documents must contain a root element. This element is"the parent" of all other elements. The elements in an XML document form a document tree. The tree starts at the root and branches to the lowest level of the tree.

All elements can have sub elements (child elements):

```
<root>
  <child>
    <subchild>.....</subchild>
  </child>
</root>
```

The terms parent, child, and sibling are used to describe the relationships between elements. Parent elements have children. Children on the same level are called siblings (brothers or sisters). All elements can have text content and attributes (just like in HTML).

ML SYNTAX RULES

The syntax rules of XML are very simple and logical. The rules are easy to learn, and easy to use.

All XML Elements Must Have a Closing Tag

In HTML, you will often see elements that don't have a closing tag:

```
<p>This is a paragraph
<p>This is another paragraph
```

In XML, it is illegal to omit the closing tag. All elements must have a closing tag:

```
<p>This is a paragraph</p>
<p>This is another paragraph</p>
```

Note: You might have noticed from the previous example that the XML declaration did not have a closing tag. This is not an error. The declaration is not a part of the XML document itself, and it has no closing tag.

XML Tags are Case Sensitive

XML elements are defined using XML tags.

XML tags are case sensitive. With XML, the tag <Letter> is different from the tag <letter>.

Opening and closing tags must be written with the same case:

```
<Message>This is incorrect</message>
<message>This is correct</message>
```

Note:"Opening and closing tags" are often referred to as"Start and end tags". Use whatever you prefer. It is exactly the same thing.

XML Elements Must be Properly Nested

In HTML, you might see improperly nested elements:

```
<b><i>This text is bold and italic</b></i>
```

In XML, all elements must be properly nested within each other:

```
<b><i>This text is bold and italic</i></b>
```

In the example above,"Properly nested" simply means that since the <i> element is opened inside the <b> element, it must be closed inside the <b> element.

XML Documents Must Have a Root Element

XML documents must contain one element that is the parent of all other elements. This element is called the root element.

```
<root>
  <child>
   <subchild>.....</subchild>
  </child>
</root>
```

XML Attribute Values Must be Quoted

XML elements can have attributes in name/value pairs just like in HTML. In XML the attribute value must always be quoted. Study the two XML documents below.

The first one is incorrect, the second is correct:

```
<note date=12/11/2007>
  <to>Tove</to>
  <from>Jani</from>
</note>
```

The error in the first document is that the date attribute in the note element is not quoted.

Entity References

Some characters have a special meaning in XML.

If you place a character like"<" inside an XML element, it will generate an error because the parser interprets it as the start of a new element.

This will generate an XML error:

```
<message>if salary < 1000 then</message>
```

To avoid this error, replace the"<" character with an entity reference:

```
<message>if salary &lt; 1000 then</message>
```

There are 5 predefined entity references in XML:

<	<	Less than
>	>	Greater than
&	&	Ampersand
'	'	Apostrophe
"	"	Quotation mark

Note: Only the characters"<" and"and" are strictly illegal in XML. The greater than character is legal, but it is a good habit to replace it.

Comments in XML

The syntax for writing comments in XML is similar to that of HTML.

```
<!-- This is a comment -->
```

White-space is Preserved in XML

HTML truncates multiple white-space characters to one single white-space:

HTML:	Hello my name is Tove
Output:	Hello my name is Tove.

With XML, the white-space in a document is not truncated.

XML Stores New Line as LF

In Windows applications, a new line is normally stored as a pair of characters: carriage return (CR) and line feed (LF). The character pair bears some resemblance to the typewriter actions of setting a new line.

In Unix applications, a new line is normally stored as a LF character. Macintosh applications also use an LF to store a new line.

XML ELEMENT

What is an XML Element

An XML element is everything from (including) the element's start tag to (including) the element's end tag. An element can contain other elements, simple text or a mixture of both. Elements can also have attributes.

```
<bookstore>
  <book category="CHILDREN">
    <title>Harry Potter</title>
    <author>J K. Rowling</author>
    <year>2005</year>
    <price>29.99</price>
  </book>
  <book category="WEB">
    <title>Learning XML</title>
    <author>Erik T. Ray</author>
    <year>2003</year>
    <price>39.95</price>
  </book>
</bookstore>
```

In the example above, <bookstore> and <book> have element contents, because they contain other elements. <author> has text content because it contains text.

In the example above only <book> has an attribute (category="CHILDREN").

XML Naming Rules

XML elements must follow these naming rules:

- Names can contain letters, numbers, and other characters
- Names cannot start with a number or punctuation character
- Names cannot start with the letters xml
- Names cannot contain spaces

Any name can be used, no words are reserved.

Best Naming Practices

Make names descriptive.

Names with an underscore separator are nice:

`<first_name>, <last_name>.`

Names should be short and simple, like this: <book_title> not like this:

`<the_title_of_the_book>.`

- Avoid"-" characters. If you name something"first-name," some software may think you want to subtract name from first.
- Avoid"." characters. If you name something "first.name," some software may think that"name" is a property of the object"first."
- Avoid":" characters. Colons are reserved to be used for something called namespaces (more later).

XML documents often have a corresponding database. A good practice is to use the naming rules of your database for the elements in the XML documents.

Non-English letters like éòá are perfectly legal in XML, but watch out for problems if your software vendor doesn't support them.

XML Elements are Extensible

XML elements can be extended to carry more information.

Look at the following XML example:

```
<note>
<to>Tove</to>
<from>Jani</from>
<body>Don't forget me this weekend!</body>
</note>
```

Let's imagine that we created an application that extracted the <to>, <from>, and <body> elements from the XML document to produce this output:

```
MESSAGE
To: Tove
From: Jani
Don't forget me this weekend!
```

Imagine that the author of the XML document added some extra information to it:

```
<note>
<date>2008-01-10</date>
<to>Tove</to>
<from>Jani</from>
<heading>Reminder</heading>
```

```
<body>Don't forget me this weekend!</body>
</note>
```

Should the application break or crash?

No. The application should still be able to find the <to>, <from>, and <body> elements in the XML document and produce the same output. One of the beauties of XML, is that it can often be extended without breaking applications.

XML ATTRIBUTES

From HTML you will remember this: <img src="computer.gif">. The"src" attribute provides additional information about the <img> element. In HTML (and in XML) attributes provide additional information about elements:

```
<img src="computer.gif">
<a href="demo.asp">
```

Attributes often provide information that is not a part of the data. In the example below, the file type is irrelevant to the data, but important to the software that wants to manipulate the element:

```
<file type="gif">computer.gif</file>
```

XML Attributes Must be Quoted

Attribute values must always be enclosed in quotes, but either single or double quotes can be used. For a person's sex, the person tag can be written like this:

```
<person sex="female">
```

or like this:

```
<person sex='female'>
```

If the attribute value itself contains double quotes you can use single quotes, like in this example:

```
<gangster name='George"Shotgun" Ziegler'>
```

or you can use character entities:

```
<gangster name="George andquot;Shotgunandquot; Ziegler">
```

XML Elements vs. Attributes

Take a look at these examples:

```
<person sex="female">
```

```
  <firstname>Anna</firstname>
  <lastname>Smith</lastname>
</person>
<person>
  <sex>female</sex>
  <firstname>Anna</firstname>
  <lastname>Smith</lastname>
</person>
```

In the first example sex is an attribute. In the last, sex is an element. Both examples provide the same information.

There are no rules about when to use attributes and when to use elements. Attributes are handy in HTML. In XML my advice is to avoid them. Use elements instead.

My Favourite Way

The following three XML documents contain exactly the same information:

A date attribute is used in the first example:

```
<note date="10/01/2008">
  <to>Tove</to>
  <from>Jani</from>
  <heading>Reminder</heading>
  <body>Don't forget me this weekend!</body>
</note>
```

A date element is used in the second example:

```
<note>
  <date>10/01/2008</date>
  <to>Tove</to>
  <from>Jani</from>
  <heading>Reminder</heading>
  <body>Don't forget me this weekend!</body>
</note>
```

An expanded date element is used in the third: (this is my favourite):

```
<note>
  <date>
    <day>10</day>
    <month>01</month>
```

```
   <year>2008</year>
  </date>
  <to>Tove</to>
  <from>Jani</from>
  <heading>Reminder</heading>
  <body>Don't forget me this weekend!</body>
</note>
```

Avoid XML Attributes

Some of the problems with using attributes are:

- Attributes cannot contain multiple values (elements can)
- Attributes cannot contain tree structures (elements can)
- Attributes are not easily expandable (for future changes)

Attributes are difficult to read and maintain. Use elements for data. Use attributes for information that is not relevant to the data.

Don't end up like this:

```
<note day="10" month="01" year="2008"
to="Tove" from="Jani" heading="Reminder"
body="Don't forget me this weekend!">
</note>
```

XML Attributes for Metadata

Sometimes ID references are assigned to elements. These IDs can be used to identify XML elements in much the same way as the ID attribute in HTML.

This example demonstrates this:

```
<messages>
  <note id="501">
   <to>Tove</to>
   <from>Jani</from>
   <heading>Reminder</heading>
   <body>Don't forget me this weekend!</body>
  </note>
  <note id="502">
```

```
    <to>Jani</to>
    <from>Tove</from>
    <heading>Re: Reminder</heading>
    <body>I will not</body>
  </note>
</messages>
```

The ID above is just an identifier, to identify the different notes. It is not a part of the note itself. What I'm trying to say here is that metadata (data about data) should be stored as attributes, and that data itself should be stored as elements.

XML VALIDATION

XML with correct syntax is"Well Formed" XML.
XML validated against a DTD is"Valid" XML.

WELL FORMED XML DOCUMENTS

A"Well Formed" XML document has correct XML syntax.
The syntax rules were described as:

- XML documents must have a root element
- XML elements must have a closing tag
- XML tags are case sensitive
- XML elements must be properly nested
- XML attribute values must be quoted

```
<?xml version="1.0" encoding="ISO-8859-1"?>
<note>
<to>Tove</to>
<from>Jani</from>
<heading>Reminder</heading>
<body>Don't forget me this weekend!</body>
</note>
```

Valid XML Documents

A"Valid" XML document is a"Well Formed" XML document, which also conforms to the rules of a Document Type Definition (DTD):

```
<?xml version="1.0" encoding="ISO-8859-1"?>
<!DOCTYPE note SYSTEM"Note.dtd">
<note>
```

```
<to>Tove</to>
<from>Jani</from>
<heading>Reminder</heading>
<body>Don't forget me this weekend!</body>
</note>
```

The DOCTYPE declaration in the example above, is a reference to an external DTD file. The content of the file is shown in the paragraph below.

XML DTD

The purpose of a DTD is to define the structure of an XML document. It defines the structure with a list of legal elements:

```
<!DOCTYPE note
[
<!ELEMENT note (to,from,heading,body)>
<!ELEMENT to (#PCDATA)>
<!ELEMENT from (#PCDATA)>
<!ELEMENT heading (#PCDATA)>
<!ELEMENT body (#PCDATA)>
]>
```

If you want to study DTD, you will find our DTD tutorial on our homepage.

XML Schema

W3C supports an XML-based alternative to DTD, called XML Schema:

```
<xs:element name="note">
<xs:complexType>
  <xs:sequence>
   <xs:element name="to" type="xs:string"/>
   <xs:element name="from" type="xs:string"/>
   <xs:element name="heading" type="xs:string"/>
   <xs:element name="body" type="xs:string"/>
   </xs:sequence>
  </xs:complexType>
</xs:element>
```

If you want to study XML Schema, you will find our Schema tutorial on our homepage.

A General XML Validator

To help you check the syntax of your XML files, we have created an XML validator to syntax-check your XML.

XML VALIDATOR

Use our XML validator to syntax-check your XML.

XML Errors Will Stop You

Errors in XML documents will stop your XML applications. The W3C XML specification states that a programme should stop processing an XML document if it finds an error. The reason is that XML software should be small, fast, and compatible.

HTML browsers will display documents with errors (like missing end tags). HTML browsers are big and incompatible because they have a lot of unnecessary code to deal with (and display) HTML errors. With XML, errors are not allowed.

Syntax-Check Your XML

To help you syntax-check your XML, we have created an XML validator. Paste your XML into the text area below, and syntax-check it by clicking the"Validate" button.

<?xml version="1.0" ?> <note> <to>Tove</to> <from>Jani</ Ffrom> <heading>Reminder</heading> <body>Don't forget me this weekend!</body> </note>

Note: This only checks if your XML is"Well formed". If you want to validate your XML against a DTD, see the last paragraph on this page.

Syntax-Check an XML File

You can syntax-check an XML file by typing the URL of the file into the input field below, and then click the"Validate" button:

Note: If you get an"Access denied" error, it's because your browser security does not allow file access across domains.

The file"note_error.xml" demonstrates your browsers error handling. If you want see an error free message, substitute the"note_error.xml" with"cd_catalog.xml".

Validate Your XML Against a DTD

If you know DTD, you can validate your XML in the text area below. Just add the DOCTYPE declaration to your XML and click the"Validate" button:

VIEWING XML FILES

```
<?xml version="1.0" encoding="ISO-8859-1"?>
  - <note>
    <to>Tove</to>
    <from>Jani</from>
    <heading>Reminder</heading>
    <body>Don't forget me this weekend!</body>
</note>
```

Look at this XML file: Note.xml The XML document will be displayed with colour-coded root and child elements. A plus (+) or minus sign (-) to the left of the elements can be clicked to expand or collapse the element structure. To view the raw XML source (without the + and–signs), select"View Page Source" or"View Source" from the browser menu.

Note: In Chrome, Opera, and Safari, only the element text will be displayed. To view the raw XML, you must right click the page and select"View Source"

Viewing an Invalid XML File

If an erroneous XML file is opened, the browser will report the error.

Look at this XML file: note_error.xml

Other XML Examples

Viewing some XML documents will help you get the XML feeling:

- An XML CD catalog
- This is a CD collection, stored as XML data.
- An XML plant catalog
- This is a plant catalog from a plant shop, stored as XML data.
- A Simple Food Menu

- This is a breakfast food menu from a restaurant, stored as XML data.

Why Does XML Display Like This

XML documents do not carry information about how to display the data. Since XML tags are"invented" by the author of the XML document, browsers do not know if a tag like <table> describes an HTML table or a dining table.

Without any information about how to display the data, most browsers will just display the XML document as it is. In this we will take a look at different solutions to the display problem, using CSS, XSLT and JavaScript.

DISPLAYING XML WITH CSS

With CSS (Cascading Style Sheets) you can add display information to an XML document.

Displaying your XML Files with CSS

It is possible to use CSS to format an XML document. Below is an example of how to use a CSS style sheet to format an XML document:

Take a look at this XML file: The CD catalog

Then look at this style sheet: The CSS file

Finally, view: The CD catalog formatted with the CSS file

Below is a fraction of the XML file. The second line links the XML file to the CSS file:

```
<?xml version="1.0" encoding="ISO-8859-1"?>
<?xml-stylesheettype="text/css"href="cd_
catalog.css"?>
<CATALOG>
  <CD>
    <TITLE>Empire Burlesque</TITLE>
    <ARTIST>Bob Dylan</ARTIST>
    <COUNTRY>USA</COUNTRY>
    <COMPANY>Columbia</COMPANY>
    <PRICE>10.90</PRICE>
    <YEAR>1985</YEAR>
  </CD>
```

```
<CD>
  <TITLE>Hide your heart</TITLE>
  <ARTIST>Bonnie Tyler</ARTIST>
  <COUNTRY>UK</COUNTRY>
  <COMPANY>CBS Records</COMPANY>
  <PRICE>9.90</PRICE>
  <YEAR>1988</YEAR>
</CD>
.
.
.
</CATALOG>
```

Formatting XML with CSS is not the most common . W3C recommend using XSLT instead.

DISPLAYING XML WITH XSLT

XSLT is the recommended style sheet language of XML. XSLT (eXtensible Stylesheet Language Transformations) is far more sophisticated than CSS.

XSLT can be used to transform XML into HTML, before it is displayed by a browser: Display XML with XSLT If you want to learn more about XSLT, find our XSLT tutorial on our homepage.

Transforming XML with XSLT on the Server

In the example above, the XSLT transformation is done by the browser, when the browser reads the XML file. Different browsers may produce different result when transforming XML with XSLT. To reduce this problem the XSLT transformation can be done on the server.

View the result:

Note: that the result of the output is exactly the same, either the transformation is done by the web server or by the web browser.

XML JAVASCRIPT

With an XMLHttpRequest you can communicate with your server from inside a web page.

WHAT IS THE XMLHTTPREQUEST OBJECT

The XMLHttpRequest object is the developer's dream, because you can:

- Update a web page with new data without reloading the page
- Request and receive new data from a server after the page has loaded
- Communicate with a server in the background

Creating an XMLHttp Request Object

Creating an XMLHttpRequest object is done with one single line of JavaScript.

In all modern browsers:

```
var xmlhttp=new XMLHttpRequest()
```

In older Microsoft browsers (IE 5 and 6):

```
var xmlhttp=new ActiveXObject("Microsoft.XMLHTTP")
```

In this, we will use the XMLHttpRequest object to retrieve XML information from a server.

Is the XMLHttpRequest Object a W3C Standard

The XMLHttpRequest object is not specified in any W3C recommendation. However, the W3C DOM Level 3"Load and Save" specification contains some similar functionality, but these are not implemented in any browsers yet.

XML PARSER

The XML DOM contains methods (functions) to traverse XML trees, access, insert, and delete nodes. However, before an XML document can be accessed and manipulated, it must be loaded into an XML DOM object. An XML parser reads XML, and converts it into an XML DOM object that can be accessed with JavaScript. Most browsers have a built-in XML parser.

Access Across Domains

For security reasons, modern browsers do not allow access across domains. This means, that both the web page and the XML file it tries to load, must be located on the same server.

The examples on W3Schools all open XML files located on the W3Schools domain. If you want to use the example above on one of your web pages, the XML files you load must be located on your own server.

THE XML DOM

The XML DOM (XML Document Object Model) defines a standard way for accessing and manipulating XML documents. The DOM views XML documents as a tree-structure. All elements can be accessed through the DOM tree. Their content (text and attributes) can be modified or deleted, and new elements can be created. The elements, their text, and their attributes are all known as nodes.

In the examples below we use the following DOM reference to get the text from the <to> element,

xmlDoc. get Elements By Tag Name ("to") [0]. child Nodes[0].nodeValue:

- XmlDoc–the XML document created by the parser.
- Get ElementsByTagName("to")[0]–the first <to> element
- Child Nodes[0]–the first child of the <to> element (the text node)
- Node Value–the value of the node (the text itself)

You can learn more about the XML DOM in our XML DOM tutorial.

The HTML DOM

The HTML DOM (HTML Document Object Model) defines a standard way for accessing and manipulating HTML documents. All HTML elements can be accessed through the HTML DOM. In the examples below we use the following DOM reference to change the text of the HTML element where id="to":

Document.getElementById("to").innerHTML:

- Document–the HTML document
- GetElementById("to")–the HTML element where id="to"
- InnerHTML–the inner text of the HTML element

You can learn more about the HTML DOM in our HTML DOM tutorial.

Load an XML File - A Cross browser Example

```
<html>
<body>
<h1>W3Schools Internal Note</h1>
<p><b>To:</b> <span id="to"></span><br/>
<b>From:</b> <span id="from"></span><br/>
<b>Message:</b> <span id="message"></span>
<script type="text/javascript">
if (window.XMLHttpRequest)
  {
  xhttp=new XMLHttpRequest()
  }
else
  {
  xhttp=new ActiveXObject("Microsoft.XMLHTTP")
}

xhttp.open("GET","note.xml",false);
xhttp.send("");
xmlDoc=xhttp.responseXML;
document.getElementById("to").innerHTML=
xmlDoc.getElementsByTagName("to")[0].childNodes[0].nodeValue;
document.getElementById("from").innerHTML=
xmlDoc.getElementsByTagName("from")[0].childNodes[0].nodeValue;
document.getElementById("message").innerHTML=
xmlDoc.getElementsByTagName("body")[0].childNodes
[0].nodeValue;
</script>
</body>
</html>
```

Example: The following code loads an XML document ("note.xml") into the XML parser:

Important Note

To extract the text"Jani" from the XML, the syntax is:

```
getElementsByTagName("from")[0].childNodes[0].
nodeValue
```

In the XML example there is only one <from> tag, but you still have to specify the array index [0], because the XML parser method getElementsByTagName() returns an array of all <from> nodes.

Example Explained

- We check the browser, and load the XML using the correct parser.
- We create an HTML table with <table border="1">
- We use getElements By Tag Name() to get all XML CD nodes
- For each CD node, we display data from ARTIST and TITLE as table data.
- We end the table with </table>

XML APPLICATION

The XML Example Document

Look at the following XML document ("cd_catalog.xml"), that represents a CD catalog:

```
<?xml version="1.0" encoding="ISO-8859-1"?>
<CATALOG>
  <CD>
   <Title>Empire Burlesque</Title>
   <Artist>Bob Dylan</Artist>
   <COUNTRY>USA</COUNTRY>
   <COMPANY>Columbia</COMPANY>
   <PRICE>10.90</PRICE>
   <YEAR>1985</YEAR>
  </CD>
.
.
```

Load the XML Document

To load the XML document (cd_catalog.xml), we use the same code as we used in the XML Parser,

```
if (window.XMLHttpRequest)
  {
  xhttp=new XMLHttpRequest();
  }
else// Internet Explorer 5/6
  {
  xhttp=new ActiveXObject("Microsoft.XMLHTTP");
  }
xhttp.open("GET","cd_catalog.xml",false);
xhttp.send("");
xmlDoc=xhttp.responseXML;
```

After the execution of this code, xmlDoc is an XML DOM object, accessible by JavaScript.

All Together Now

With a little creativity you can create a full application.

If you use what you have learned on this page, and a little imagination, you can easily develop this into a full application.

XML ADVANCED

XML NAMESPACES

Name Conflicts

In XML, element names are defined by the developer. This often results in a conflict when trying to mix XML documents from different XML applications.

This XML carries HTML table information:

```
<table>
  <tr>
   <td>Apples</td>
   <td>Bananas</td>
  </tr>
</table>
```

This XML carries information about a table (a piece of furniture):

```
<table>
  <name>African Coffee Table</name>
```

```
  <width>80</width>
  <length>120</length>
</table>
```

If these XML fragments were added together, there would be a name conflict. Both contain a <table> element, but the elements have different content and meaning.

An XML parser will not know how to handle these differences.

Solving the Name Conflict Using a Prefix

Name conflicts in XML can easily be avoided using a name prefix.

This XML carries information about an HTML table, and a piece of furniture:

```
<h:table>
  <h:tr>
   <h:td>Apples</h:td>
   <h:td>Bananas</h:td>
  </h:tr>
</h:table>
<f:table>
  <f:name>African Coffee Table</f:name>
  <f:width>80</f:width>
  <f:length>120</f:length>
</f:table>
```

In the example above, there will be no conflict because the two <table> elements have different names.

XML Namespaces–The xmlns Attribute

When using prefixes in XML, a so-called namespace for the prefix must be defined. The namespace is defined by the xmlns attribute in the start tag of an element.

The namespace declaration has the following syntax. xmlns:prefix="URI".

```
<root>
<h:table xmlns:h="http://www.w3.org/TR/html4/">
  <h:tr>
   <h:td>Apples</h:td>
```

```
    <h:td>Bananas</h:td>
  </h:tr>
</h:table>
<f:table xmlns:f="http://www.w3schools.com/
furniture">
  <f:name>African Coffee Table</f:name>
  <f:width>80</f:width>
  <f:length>120</f:length>
</f:table>
</root>
```

In the example above, the xmlns attribute in the <table> tag give the h: and f: prefixes a qualified namespace. When a namespace is defined for an element, all child elements with the same prefix are associated with the same namespace.

Namespaces can be declared in the elements where they are used or in the XML root element:

```
<root
xmlns:h="http://www.w3.org/TR/html4/"
xmlns:f="http://www.w3schools.com/furniture">
<h:table>
  <h:tr>
   <h:td>Apples</h:td>
   <h:td>Bananas</h:td>
  </h:tr>
</h:table>
<f:table>
  <f:name>African Coffee Table</f:name>
  <f:width>80</f:width>
  <f:length>120</f:length>
</f:table>
</root>
```

Note: The namespace URI is not used by the parser to look up information. The purpose is to give the namespace a unique name. However, often companies use the namespace as a pointer to a web page containing namespace information.

Uniform Resource Identifier (URI)

A Uniform Resource Identifier (URI) is a string of

characters which identifies an Internet Resource. The most common URI is the Uniform Resource Locator (URL) which identifies an Internet domain address. Another, not so common type of URI is the Universal Resource Name (URN). In our examples we will only use URLs.

Default Namespaces

Defining a default namespace for an element saves us from using prefixes in all the child elements. It has the following syntax:

```
xmlns="namespaceURI"
```

This XML carries HTML table information:

```
<table xmlns="http://www.w3.org/TR/html4/">
  <tr>
   <td>Apples</td>
   <td>Bananas</td>
  </tr>
</table>
```

This XML carries information about a piece of furniture:

```
<table xmlns="http://www.w3schools.com/furniture">
<name>African Coffee Table</name>
<width>80</width>
<length>120</length>
</table>
```

Namespaces in Real Use

XSLT is an XML language that can be used to transform XML documents into other formats, like HTML. In the XSLT document below, you can see that most of the tags are HTML tags. The tags that are not HTML tags have the prefix xsl, identified by the namespace xmlns:xsl="http://www.w3.org/1999/XSL/Transform":

```
<?xml version="1.0" encoding="ISO-8859-1"?>
<xsl:stylesheet version="1.0"
xmlns:xsl="http://www.w3.org/1999/XSL/Transform">
<xsl:template match="/">
<html>
<body>
```

```
  <h2>My CD Collection</h2>
  <table border="1">
   <tr>
    <th align="left">Title</th>
    <th align="left">Artist</th>
   </tr>
   <xsl:for-each select="catalog/cd">
   <tr>
    <td><xsl:value-of select="title"/></td>
    <td><xsl:value-of select="artist"/></td>
   </tr>
   </xsl:for-each>
  </table>
</body>
</html>
</xsl:template>
</xsl:stylesheet>
```

XML CDATA

All text in an XML document will be parsed by the parser.

But text inside a CDATA section will be ignored by the parser.

PCDATA–Parsed Character Data

XML parsers normally parse all the text in an XML document.

When an XML element is parsed, the text between the XML tags is also parsed:

```
<message>This text is also parsed</message>
```

The parser does this because XML elements can contain other elements, as in this example, where the <name> element contains two other elements (first and last):

```
<name><first>Bill</first><last>Gates</last></name>
```

and the parser will break it up into sub-elements like this:

```
<name>
  <first>Bill</first>
  <last>Gates</last>
</name>
```

Parsed Character Data (PCDATA) is a term used about text data that will be parsed by the XML parser.

CDATA–(Unparsed) Character Data

The term CDATA is used about text data that should not be parsed by the XML parser.

Characters like"<" and"and" are illegal in XML elements:

- "<" will generate an error because the parser interprets it as the start of a new element.
- "&" will generate an error because the parser interprets it as the start of an character entity.

Some text, like JavaScript code, contains a lot of"<" or"and" characters. To avoid errors script code can be defined as CDATA.

Everything inside a CDATA section is ignored by the parser. A CDATA section starts with"<![CDATA[" and ends with"]]>":

```
<script>
<![CDATA[
function matchwo(a,b)
{
if (a < b && a < 0) then
  {
  return 1;
  }
else
  {
  return 0;
  }
}
]]>
</script>
```

In the example above, everything inside the CDATA section is ignored by the parser.

Notes on CDATA Sections

A CDATA section cannot contain the string"]]>". Nested CDATA sections are not allowed.

The"]]>" that marks the end of the CDATA section cannot contain spaces or line breaks.

XML ENCODING

XML documents can contain non ASCII characters, like Norwegian æ ø å, or French ê è é.

To avoid errors, specify the XML encoding, or save XML files as Unicode.

XML Encoding Errors

If you load an XML document, you can get two different errors indicating encoding problems: An invalid character was found in text content. You get this error if your XML contains non ASCII characters, and the file was saved as single-byte ANSI (or ASCII) with no encoding specified.

- Single byte XML file with encoding attribute.
- Same single byte XML file with no encoding attribute.
- Switch from current encoding to specified encoding not supported.

You get this error if your XML file was saved as double-byte Unicode (or UTF-16) with a single-byte encoding (Windows-1252, ISO-8859-1, UTF-8) specified.

You also get this error if your XML file was saved with single-byte ANSI (or ASCII), with double-byte encoding (UTF-16) specified. Double byte XML file without encoding. Same double byte XML file with single byte encoding.

Windows Notepad

Windows Notepad save files as single-byte ANSI (ASCII) by default. If you select"Save as...", you can specify double-byte Unicode (UTF-16). Save the XML file below as Unicode (note that the document does not contain any encoding attribute):

```
<?xml version="1.0"?>
<note>
<from>Jani</from>
<to>Tove</to>
<message>Norwegian: æøå. French: êèé</message>
```

```
</note>
```

The file above, note_encode_none_u.xml will NOT generate an error. But if you specify a single-byte encoding it will.

The following encoding (open it), will give an error message:

```
<?xml version="1.0" encoding="windows-1252"?>
```

The following encoding (open it), will give an error message:

```
<?xml version="1.0" encoding="ISO-8859-1"?>
```

The following encoding (open it), will give an error message:

```
<?xml version="1.0" encoding="UTF-8"?>
```

The following encoding (open it), will NOT give an error:

```
<?xml version="1.0" encoding="UTF-16"?>
```

Conclusion

- Always use the encoding attribute
- Use an editor that supports encoding
- Make sure you know what encoding the editor uses
- Use the same encoding in your encoding attribute

XML ON THE SERVER

XML files are plain text files just like HTML files.

XML can easily be stored and generated by a standard web server.

Storing XML Files on the Server

XML files can be stored on an Internet server exactly the same way as HTML files.

Start Windows Notepad and write the following lines:

```
<?xml version="1.0" encoding="ISO-8859-1"?>
<note>
  <from>Jani</from>
  <to>Tove</to>
  <message>Remember me this weekend</message>
</note>
```

Save the file on your web server with a proper name like"note.xml".

Generating XML with ASP

XML can be generated on a server without any installed XML software. To generate an XML response from the server–simply write the following code and save it as an ASP file on the web server:

```
<%
response.ContentType="text/xml"
response.Write("<?xml version='1.0' encoding='ISO-8859-1'?>")
response.Write("<note>")
response.Write("<from>Jani</from>")
response.Write("<to>Tove</to>")
response.Write("<message>Remember me this weekend</message>")
response.Write("</note>")
%>
```

Note that the content type of the response must be set to"text/xml". See how the ASP file will be returned from the server. If you want to study ASP, you will find our ASP tutorial on our homepage.

Generating XML with PHP

To generate an XML response from the server using PHP, use following code:

```
<?php
header("Content-type: text/xml");
echo"<?xml version='1.0' encoding='ISO-8859-1'?>";
echo"<note>";
echo"<from>Jani</from>";
echo"<to>Tove</to>";
echo"<message>Remember me this weekend</message>";
echo"</note>";
?>
```

Note that the content type of the response header must be set to"text/xml".

Generating XML From a Database

XML can be generated from a database without any

installed XML software. To generate an XML database response from the server, simply write the following code and save it as an ASP file on the web server:

```
<%
response.ContentType ="text/xml"
set conn=Server.CreateObject("ADODB.Connection")
conn.provider="Microsoft.Jet.OLEDB.4.0;"
conn.open server.mappath("/db/database.mdb")
sql="select fname,lname from tblGuestBook"
set rs=Conn.Execute(sql)
response.write("<?xml version='1.0' encoding='ISO-
8859-1'?>")
response.write("<guestbook>")
while (not rs.EOF)
response.write("<guest>")
response.write("<fname>" and rs("fname") and"</
fname>")
response.write("<lname>" and rs("lname") and"</
lname>")
response.write("</guest>")
rs.MoveNext()
wend
rs.close()
conn.close()
response.write("</guestbook>")
%>
```

The example above uses ASP with ADO. If you want to study ASP and ADO, you will find the tutorials on our homepage.

Transforming XML with XSLT on the Server

This ASP transforms an XML file to XHTML on the server:

```
<%
'Load XML
set xml = Server.CreateObject("Microsoft.XMLDOM")
xml.async = false
xml.load(Server.MapPath("simple.xml"))
'Load XSL
```

```
set xsl = Server.CreateObject("Microsoft.XMLDOM")
xsl.async = false
xsl.load(Server.MapPath("simple.xsl"))
'Transform file
Response.Write(xml.transformNode(xsl))
%>
```

Example explained:

- The first block of code creates an instance of the Microsoft XML parser (XMLDOM), and loads the XML file into memory.
- The second block of code creates another instance of the parser and loads the XSL file into memory.
- The last line of code transforms the XML document using the XSL document, and sends the result as XHTML to your browser. Nice!

Saving XML To a File Using ASP

This ASP example creates a simple XML document and saves it on the server:

```
<%
text="<note>"
text=text and"<to>Tove</to>"
text=text and"<from>Jani</from>"
text=text and"<heading>Reminder</heading>"
text=text and"<body>Don't forget me this
weekend!</body>"

text=text and"</note>"
set xmlDoc=Server.CreateObject("Microsoft.XMLDOM")
xmlDoc.async="false"
xmlDoc.loadXML(text)
xmlDoc.Save("test.xml")
%>
```

XML DOM ADVANCED

The XML DOM (Document Object Model) defines a standard way for accessing and manipulating XML documents.

The XML DOM

The DOM views XML documents as a tree-structure. All elements can be accessed through the DOM tree. Their content (text and attributes) can be modified or deleted, and new elements can be created. The elements, their text, and their attributes are all known as nodes.

In this we introduced the XML DOM, and used the XML DOM get Elements ByTagName() method to retrieve data from a DOM tree.

In this we will describe some other commonly used XML DOM methods. In the examples below, we have used the XML file: books.xml.

Get the Value of an Element

The following code retrieves the text value of the first <title> element:

Example:

```
x=xml Doc. get Elements By Tag Name ("title")
[0].child Nodes[0];
txt=x.node Value;
```

Get the Value of an Attribute

The following code retrieves the text value of the"lang" attribute of the first <title> element:

Example

```
txt=xmlDoc.getElementsBy Tag Name("title")[0].get
Attribute("lang");
```

Change the Value of an Element

The following code changes the text value of the first <title> element:

Example:

```
x=xmlDoc.get Elements By Tag Name
("title")[0].child Nodes[0];
x.nodeValue="Easy Cooking";
```

Change the Value of an Attribute

The setAttribute() method can be used to change the value of an existing attribute, or to create a new attribute.

The following code adds a new attribute called"edition" (with the value"first") to each <book> element:

Example:

```
x=xmlDoc.getElementsByTagName("book");
for(i=0;i<x.length;i++)
{
x[i].setAttribute("edition","first");
}
```

Create an Element

The createElement() method creates a new element node.

The createTextNode() method creates a new text node.

The appendChild() method adds a child node to a node (after the last child).

To create a new element with text content, it is necessary to create both an element node and a text node.

The following code creates an element (<edition>), and adds it to the first <book> element:

Example:

```
newel=xmlDoc.createElement("edition");
newtext=xmlDoc.createTextNode("First");
newel.appendChild(newtext);
x=xmlDoc.getElementsByTagName("book");
x[0].appendChild(newel);
```

Example explained:

```
" Create an <edition> element
" Create a text node with value ="First"
" Append the text node to the <edition> element
" Append the <edition> element to the first <book>
element
```

Remove an Element

The removeChild() method removes a specified node (or element). The following code fragment will remove the first node in the first <book> element:

Example:

```
x=xmlDoc.getElementsByTagName("book")[0];
x.removeChild(x.childNodes[0]);
```

Note: The result of the example above may be different depending on what browser you use. Firefox treats new lines as empty text nodes, Internet Explorer don't. You can read more about this and how to avoid it in the XML DOM tutorial.

XML DON'T

Here are some technologies you should try to avoid when using XML.

Internet Explorer–XML Data Islands

What is it? An XML data island is XML data embedded into an HTML page. Why avoid it? XML Data Islands only works with Internet Explorer browsers. What to use instead? You should use JavaScript and XML DOM to parse and display XML in HTML.

For more information about JavaScript and XML DOM, visit our XML DOM tutorial.

XML Data Island Example

This example uses the XML document"cd_catalog.xml".

Bind the XML document to an <xml> tag in the HTML document. The id attribute defines an id for the data island, and the src attribute points to the XML file:

Example:

This example only works in IE

```
<html>
<body>
<xml id="cdcat" src="cd_catalog.xml"></xml>
<table border="1" datasrc="#cdcat">
<tr>
<td><span datafld="ARTIST"></span></td>
<td><span datafld="TITLE"></span></td>
</tr>
</table>
</body>
</html>
```

The datasrc attribute of the <table> tag binds the HTML table to the XML data island. The <span> tags allow the datafld attribute to refer to the XML element to be displayed. In this case,"ARTIST" and"TITLE". As the XML is read, additional rows are created for each <CD> element.

XML EDITORS

If you are serious about XML, you will benefit from using a professional XML Editor.

XML is Text-based

XML is a text-based markup language. One great thing about XML is that XML files can be created and edited using a simple text-editor like Notepad.

However, when you start working with XML, you will soon find that it is better to edit XML documents using a professional XML editor.

Why Not Notepad

Many web developers use Notepad to edit both HTML and XML documents because Notepad is included with the most common OS and it is simple to use. Personally I often use Notepad for quick editing of simple HTML, CSS, and XML files. But, if you use Notepad for XML editing, you will soon run into problems. Notepad does not know that you are writing XML, so it will not be able to assist you.

Why an XML Editor

Today XML is an important technology, and development projects use XML-based technologies like:

- XML Schema to define XML structures and data types
- XSLT to transform XML data
- SOAP to exchange XML data between applications
- WSDL to describe web services
- RDF to describe web resources
- XPath and XQuery to access XML data
- SMIL to define graphics

To be able to write error-free XML documents, you will need an intelligent XML editor!

XML Editors

Professional XML editors will help you to write error-free XML documents, validate your XML against a DTD or a schema, and force you to stick to a valid XML structure.

An XML editor should be able to:

- Add closing tags to your opening tags automatically
- Force you to write valid XML
- Verify your XML against a DTD
- Verify your XML against a Schema
- Colour code your XML syntax

At W3Schools we have been using XMLSpy for many years. XMLSpy is our favourite XML editor.

These are some of the features we especially like:

- Easy to use
- Context-sensitive entry helpers
- Syntax colouring and pretty printing
- Built in validation and well-formedness checking
- Easy switching between text view and grid view
- Graphical XML Schema editor
- Database import and export for all major databases
- Built in templates for many XML document types
- Intelligent XPath 1.0/2.0 auto-completion
- XSLT 1.0/2.0 editor, profiler, and debugger
- XQuery editor, profiler, and debugger
- SOAP client and debugger
- Graphical WSDL editor
- XBRL validation and taxonomy editing
- Support for Office 2007/ OOXML
- Code generation in Java, C++, and C#

A CONCRETE VIEW OF XML

An XML document is a (Unicode) text with markup tags and other meta-information.

An XML document must be well-formed:

- Start and end tags must match
- Element tags must be properly nested
- + some more subtle syntactical requirements

Note: XML is case sensitive!

Special characters can be escaped using Unicode character references:

- < and < both yield <
- & and & both yield &

CDATA Sections are an alternative to escaping many characters:

```
<![CDATA[<greeting>Hello, world!</greeting>]]>
```

The strange syntax is a legacy from SGML...

White-space (blanks, newlines, etc.) is used both for indentation and actual contents. (xml:space attribute provides some control.)

Other meta-information:

```
<?target data...?>
```

an instruction for a processor, target identifies the processor for which it is directed, data is a string containing the instruction

```
<!-- comment -->
```

a comment, will be ignored by all processors

```
<!DOCTYPE...>
```

THE RECIPE EXAMPLE

Consider again recipes, such as in this example (raw text file).

We design an XML version of a recipe collection:

- Recipes consist of ingredients, steps for preparation, possibly some comments, and a specification of its nutrition
- An ingredient can be simple or composite
- A simple ingredient has a name, an amount (possibly unspecified), an a unit (unless amount is dimensionless)
- A composite ingredient is recursively a recipe with ingredients and preparation

FROM SGML TO SML

DocHeads vs. Simpletons, a process of simplification SGML (Standard Generalized Markup Language)

- ISO standard, 1985
- Huge amount of"document archive" applications in government, military, industry, academia...
- A successfull well-known application: HTML is designed as a simple application of SGML.

|
V

XML

- W3C Recommendation 1998
- A simple subset of SGML, targeted for Web applications
- Now de facto standard

|
V

MinML (Minimal XML, previously known as SML–Simple Markup Language)

- Web community discussions and collaborations, started 1999
- Simplifies the XML spec: no DTDs, processing instructions, or comments, UTF-8 and UTF-16 only, considerations on element attributes, white-space...

Canonical XML

- W3C Recommendation, March 2001
- Intended as simplification of general XML documents, not as a simplified XML spec
- "Xanonical" representation
- Removes document type declarations, imposes ordering on attributes, UTF-8 encoding, etc.

XML TECHNOLOGIES

XML is:

- Hot ($$$)
- The standard for representation of Web information
- By itself, just a notation for hierarchically structured text

But a notation for tree structures is not enough:

- The real force of XML is generic languages and tools!

- By building on XML, you get a massive infrastructure for free

The XML vision offers:

- Common extensions to the core XML specification
  - A namespace mechanism, document inclusion, etc.
- Schemas
  - Grammars to define classes of documents
- linking between documents
  - A generalization of HTML anchors and links
- Addressing parts of read-only documents
  - Flexible and robust pointers into documents
- Transformation
  - Conversion from one document class to another
- Querying
  - Extraction of information, generalizing relational databases

To"use XML":

- Define your XML language (use *e.g.* XML Schema to define its syntax)
- Exploit the generic XML tools (*e.g.* XSLT and XQuery processors), the generic protocols, and the generic programming frameworks (*e.g.* DOM or SAX) to build application tools.

2

Markup Languages

HTML

DESCRIPTION

What is Hyper-text

- A document that contains links to other documents (and text, sound, images...)
- Links may be actuated automatically or on request
- Linked documents may replace, be inlined, or create a new window
- Most combinations are supported by HTML

What is a Markup Language

- A notation for writing text with markup tags
- The tags indicate the structure of the text
- Tags have names and attributes
- Tags may enclose a part of the text

HTML

Exchange data on the Internet:

- Documents are published by servers
- Documents are presented by clients (browsers)

HTML was created by Tim Berners-Lee and Robert Caillau at CERN in 1991:

MOTIVATION

The motivation was to keep track of experimental data

HTML describes only the logical structure of documents:

- Browsers are free to interpret markup tags as they please
- The document even makes sense if the tags are ignored

HTML combined well-known ideas:

- Hyper-text was known since 1945
- Markup languages date back to 1970

A hand conversion to HTML of the original MacWord (or Word for Mac?) document written in March 1989 and later redistributed unchanged apart from the date added in May 1990. Provided for historical interest only. The diagrams are a bit dotty, but available in versioins linked below. The text has not been changed, even to correct errors such as misnumbered figures or unfinished references.

This document was an attempt to persuade CERN management that a global hypertext system was in CERN's interests. Note that the only name I had for it at this time was"Mesh" -- I decided on"World Wide Web" when writing the code in 1990.

Overview

Many of the discussions of the future at CERN and the LHC era end with the question–ªYes, but how will we ever keep track of such a large project?º This proposal provides an answer to such questions. Firstly, it discusses the problem of information access at CERN. Then, it introduces the idea of linked information systems, and compares them with less flexible ways of finding information.

It then summarises my short experience with non-linear text systems known as ªhypertextº, describes what CERN needs from such a system, and what industry may provide. Finally, it suggests steps we should take to involve ourselves with hypertext now, so that individually and collectively we may understand what we are creating.

Losing Information at CERN

CERN is a wonderful organisation. It involves several

thousand people, many of them very creative, all working towards common goals. Although they are nominally organised into a hierarchical management structure,this does not constrain the way people will communicate, and share information, equipment and software across groups.

The actual observed working structure of the organisation is a multiply connected"web" whose interconnections evolve with time. In this environment, a new person arriving, or someone taking on a new task, is normally given a few hints as to who would be useful people to talk to. Information about what facilities exist and how to find out about them travels in the corridor gossip and occasional newsletters, and the details about what is required to be done spread in a similar way. All things considered, the result is remarkably successful, despite occasional misunderstandings and duplicated effort.

A problem, however, is the high turnover of people. When two years is a typical length of stay, information is constantly being lost. The introduction of the new people demands a fair amount of their time and that of others before they have any idea of what goes on. The technical details of past projects are sometimes lost forever, or only recovered after a detective investigation in an emergency. Often, the information has been recorded, it just cannot be found.

If a CERN experiment were a static once-only development, all the information could be written in a big book. As it is, CERN is constantly changing as new ideas are produced, as new technology becomes available, and in order to get around unforeseen technical problems. When a change is necessary, it normally affects only a small part of the organisation. A local reason arises for changing a part of the experiment or detector. At this point, one has to dig around to find out what other parts and people will be affected. Keeping a book up to date becomes impractical, and the structure of the book needs to be constantly revised.

The sort of information we are discussing answers, for example, questions like:

- Where is this module used?
- Who wrote this code? Where does he work?

- What documents exist about that concept?
- Which laboratories are included in that project?
- Which systems depend on this device?
- What documents refer to this one?

The problems of information loss may be particularly acute at CERN, but in this case (as in certain others), CERN is a model in miniature of the rest of world in a few years time. CERN meets now some problems which the rest of the world will have to face soon. In 10 years, there may be many commercial solutions to the problems above, while today we need something to allow us to continue.

Linked Information Systems

In providing a system for manipulating this sort of information, the hope would be to allow a pool of information to develop which could grow and evolve with the organisation and the projects it describes. For this to be possible, the method of storage must not place its own restraints on the information. This is why a"web" of notes with links (like references) between them is far more useful than a fixed hierarchical system. When describing a complex system, many people resort to diagrams with circles and arrows. Circles and arrows leave one free to describe the interrelationships between things in a way that tables, for example, do not. The system we need is like a diagram of circles and arrows, where circles and arrows can stand for anything.

We can call the circles nodes, and the arrows links. Suppose each node is like a small note, summary article, or comment. I'm not over concerned here with whether it has text or graphics or both. Ideally, it represents or describes one particular person or object.

Examples of nodes can be:

- People
- Software modules
- Groups of people
- Projects
- Concepts
- Documents

- Types of hardware
- Specific hardware objects

The arrows which links circle A to circle B can mean, for example, that A:

- Depends on B
- Is part of B
- Made B
- Refers to B
- Uses B
- Is an example of B

The system must allow any sort of information to be entered. Another person must be able to find the information, sometimes without knowing what he is looking for.

In practice, it is useful for the system to be aware of the generic types of the links between items (dependences, for example), and the types of nodes (people, things, documents..) without imposing any limitations.

The Problem with Trees

Many systems are organised hierarchically. The CERNDOC documentation system is an example, as is the Unix file system, and the VMS/HELP system. A tree has the practical advantage of giving every node a unique name. However, it does not allow the system to model the real world. For example, in a hierarchical HELP system such as VMS/HELP, one often gets to a leaf on a tree such as,

`HELP COMPILER SOURCE_FORMAT PRAGMAS DEFAULTS`

only to find a reference to another leaf:"Please see,

`HELP COMPILER COMMAND OPTIONS DEFAULTS PRAGMAS"`

and it is necessary to leave the system and re-enter it. What was needed was a link from one node to another, because in this case the information was not naturally organised into a tree.

Another example of a tree-structured system is the uucp News system (try'rn' under Unix). This is a hierarchical system of discussions ("newsgroups") each containing articles contributed by many people. It is a very useful method of pooling expertise, but suffers from the inflexibility of a tree.

Typically, a discussion under one newsgroup will develop into a different topic, at which point it ought to be in a different part of the tree.

The Problem with Keywords

Keywords are a common method of accessing data for which one does not have the exact coordinates. The usual problem with keywords, however, is that two people never chose the same keywords. The keywords then become useful only to people who already know the application well.

Practical keyword systems (such as that of VAX/NOTES for example) require keywords to be registered. This is already a step in the right direction. A linked system takes this to the next logical step. Keywords can be nodes which stand for a concept. A keyword node is then no different from any other node. One can link documents, etc., to keywords. One can then find keywords by finding any node to which they are related. In this way, documents on similar topics are indirectly linked, through their key concepts. A keyword search then becomes a search starting from a small number of named nodes, and finding nodes which are close to all of them.

It was for these reasons that I first made a small linked information system, not realising that a term had already been coined for the idea:"hypertext".

A Solution: Hypertext

Personal Experience with Hypertext

In 1980, I wrote a programme for keeping track of software with which I was involved in the PS control system. Called Enquire, it allowed one to store snippets of information, and to link related pieces together in any way. To find information, one progressed via the links from one sheet to another, rather like in the old computer game"adventure". I used this for my personal record of people and modules.

Soon after my re-arrival at CERN in the DD division, I found that the environment was similar to that in PS, and I missed Enquire. I therefore produced a version for the VMS, and have used it to keep track of projects, people, groups, experiments, software modules and hardware devices with which I have worked. I have found it personally very useful. I have made no effort to make it suitable for general consumption, but have found that a few people have successfully used it to browse through the projects and find out all sorts of things of their own accord.

Hot spots

Meanwhile, several programmes have been made exploring these ideas, both commercially and academically. Most of them use"hot spots" in documents, like icons, or highlighted phrases, as sensitive areas. touching a hot spot with a mouse brings up the relevant information, or expands the text on the screen to include it. Imagine, then, the references in this document, all being associated with the network address of the thing to which they referred, so that while reading this document you could skip to them with a click of the mouse.

"Hypertext" is a term coined in the 1950s by Ted Nelson [...], which has become popular for these systems, although it is used to embrace two different ideas. One idea (which is relevant to this problem) is the concept:"Hypertext": Human-readable information linked together in an unconstrained way.

The other idea, which is independent and largely a question of technology and time, is of multimedia documents which include graphics, speech and video. I will not discuss this latter aspect further here, although I will use the word"Hypermedia" to indicate that one is not bound to text.

It has been difficult to assess the effect of a large hypermedia system on an organisation, often because these systems never had seriously large-scale use. For this reason, we require large amounts of existing information should be accessible using any new information management system.

CERN Requirements

To be a practical system in the CERN environment, there are a number of clear practical requirements.

Remote Access Across Networks.

CERN is distributed, and access from remote machines is essential.

Heterogeneity

Access is required to the same data from different types of system (VM/CMS, Macintosh, VAX/VMS, Unix)

Non-Centralisation

Information systems start small and grow. They alsc start isolated and then merge. A new system must allow existing systems to be linked together without requiring any central control or coordination.

Access to existing data: If we provide access to existing databases as though they were in hypertext form, the system will get off the ground quicker. This is discussed further below.

Private Links

One must be able to add one's own private links to and from public information. One must also be able to annotate links, as well as nodes, privately.

Bells and Whistles

Storage of ASCII text, and display on 24x80 screens, is in the short term sufficient, and essential. Addition of graphics would be an optional extra with very much less penetration for the moment.

Data Analysis

An intriguing possibility, given a large hypertext database with typed links, is that it allows some degree of automatic analysis. It is possible to search, for example, for anomalies such as undocumented software or divisions which contain no people.

It is possible to generate lists of people or devices for other purposes, such as mailing lists of people to be informed of changes. It is also possible to look at the topology of an organisation or a project, and draw conclusions about how it should be managed, and how it could evolve. This is particularly useful when the database becomes very large, and groups of projects, for example, so interwoven as to make it difficult to see the wood for the trees.

In a complex place like CERN, it's not always obvious how to divide people into groups. Imagine making a large three-dimensional model, with people represented by little spheres, and strings between people who have something in common at work.

Now imagine picking up the structure and shaking it, until you make some sense of the tangle: perhaps, you see tightly knit groups in some places, and in some places weak areas of communication spanned by only a few people. Perhaps a linked information system will allow us to see the real structure of the organisation in which we work.

Live Links

The data to which a link (or a hot spot) refers may be very static, or it may be temporary. In many cases at CERN information about the state of systems is changing all the time. Hypertext allows documents to be linked into"live" data so that every time the link is followed, the information is retrieved.

If one sacrifices portability, it is possible so make following a link fire up a special application, so that diagnostic programmes, for example, could be linked directly into the maintenance guide.

Non Requirements

Discussions on Hypertext have sometimes tackled the problem of copyright enforcement and data security. These are of secondary importance at CERN, where information exchange is still more important than secrecy.

Authorisation and accounting systems for hypertext could conceivably be designed which are very sophisticated, but they are not proposed here. In cases where reference must be made to data which is in fact protected, existing file protection systems should be sufficient.

Specific Applications

The following are three examples of specific places in which the proposed system would be immediately useful. There are many others.

Development Project Documentation

The Remote procedure Call project has a skeleton description using Enquire. Although limited, it is very useful for recording who did what, where they are, what documents exist, etc. Also, one can keep track of users, and can easily append any extra little bits of information which come to hand and have nowhere else to be put. Cross-links to other projects, and to databases which contain information on people and documents would be very useful, and save duplication of information.

Document Retrieval

The CERNDOC system provides the mechanics of storing and printing documents. A linked system would allow one to browse through concepts, documents, systems and authors, also allowing references between documents to be stored. (Once a document had been found, the existing machinery could be invoked to print it or display it).

The"Personal Skills Inventory

Personal skills and experience are just the sort of thing which need hypertext flexibility. People can be linked to projects they have worked on, which in turn can be linked to particular machines, programming languages, etc.

The State of the Art in Hypermedia

An increasing amount of work is being done into hypermedia research at universities and commercial research labs, and some commercial systems have resulted. There have been two conferences, Hypertext'87 and'88, and in Washington DC, the National Institute of Standards and Technology (NST) hosted a workshop on standardisation in hypertext, a followup of which will occur during 1990.

The Communications of the ACM special issue on Hypertext contains many references to hypertext papers. A bibliography on hypertext is given in [NIST90], and a uucp newsgroup alt.hypertext exists. I do not, therefore, give a list here.

Browsing Techniques

Much of the academic research is into the human interface side of browsing through a complex information space. Problems addressed are those of making navigation easy, and avoiding a feeling of being"lost in hyperspace".

Whilst the results of the research are interesting, many users at CERN will be accessing the system using primitive terminals, and so advanced window styles are not so important for us now.

Interconnection or Publication

Most systems available today use a single database. This is accessed by many users by using a distributed file system. There are few products which take Ted Nelson's idea of a wide"docuverse" literally by allowing links between nodes in different databases. In order to do this, some standardisation would be necessary.

However, at the standardisation workshop, the emphasis was on standardisation of the format for exchangeable media, nor for networking. This is prompted by the strong push towards publishing of hypermedia information, for example on optical disk. There seems to be a general consensus about the abstract data model which a hypertext system should use.

Many systems have been put together with little or no regard for portability, unfortunately. Some others, although published, are proprietary software which is not for external release. However, there are several interesting projects and more are appearing all the time.

Digital's"Compound Document Architecture" (CDA), for example, is a data model which may be extendible into a hypermedia model, and there are rumours that this is a way Digital would like to go.

Incentives and CALS

The US Department of Defence has given a big incentive to hypermedia research by, in effect, specifying hypermedia documentation for future procurement.

This means that all manuals for parts for defence equipment must be provided in hypermedia form. The acronym CALS stands for ªComputer-aided Acquisition and Logistic Support).

ACCESSING EXISTING DATA

The system must achieve a critical usefulness early on. Existing hypertext systems have had to justify themselves solely on new data.

If, however, there was an existing base of data of personnel, for example, to which new data could be linked, the value of each new piece of data would be greater.

In some cases, writing these servers would mean unscrambling or obtaining details of the existing protocols and/ or file formats. It may not be practical to provide the full functionality of the original system through hypertext.

In general, it will be more important to allow read access to the general public: it may be that there is a limited number of people who are providing the information, and that they are content to use the existing facilities.

It is sometimes possible to enhance an existing storage system by coding hypertext information in, if one knows that a server will be generating a hypertext representation. In'news' articles, for example, one could use (in the text) a standard format for a reference to another article.

This would be picked out by the hypertext gateway and used to generate a link to that note. This sort of enhancement will allow greater integration between old and new systems.

There will always be a large number of information management systems–we get a lot of added usefulness from being able to cross-link them.

However, we will lose out if we try to constrain them, as we will exclude systems and hamper the evolution of hypertext in general.

COMPACT AND HUMAN READABLE

Many document formats are very bulky:

- The author controls the precise layout
- All details, including many font tables, must be stored with the contents

In comparison, HTML is slim:

- The author sacrifices control for compactness
- Only the actual contents and its logical structure is represented

Compactness is good for:

- Saving space on your server
- Lowering network traffic

(Don't worry about voluminous markup–specialized compression techniques are emerging.)

Furthermore, HTML documents can be written and modified with any raw-text editor.

FROM LOGICAL TO PHYSICAL STRUCTURE

Originally, HTML tags described logical structure:

- H2:"this is a header at level 2"
- Em:"this text should be emphasized"
- Ul:"this is a list of items"

Quickly, (non-physicist) users wanted more control:

- "This header is centered and written in Times-Roman in size 28pt"
- "This text is italicized"
- "These list items are indented 7mm and use pink elephants for bullets"

The early hack for commercial pages was to make everything a huge image:

```
HTML hello.html    44 bytes
GIF hello.gif 32,700 bytes
```

The HTML developers responded with more and more physical layout tags.

STYLE SHEETS

Cascading Style Sheets (CSS):

- Specify physical properties (layout) of HTML tags

- Are (usually) written in separate files
- Can be shared for many HTML documents

There are many advantages:

- Logical and physical properties may be separated
- Document groups can have consistent looks
- The look can easily be changed

A CSS stylesheet works by:

- Allowing more than 50 properties to be defined for each kind of tag;
- The definitions for a tag may depend on its context
- Undefined properties are inherited from enclosing tags
- Normal HTML corresponds to default values of properties

Using stylesheets, all tags become logical–however, CSS stylesheets only address superficial properties of documents.

A Touch of Style offers good advice on using stylesheets.

ADDING A TOUCH OF STYLE

This is a short guide to styling your Web pages. It will show you how to use W3C's Cascading Style Sheets language (CSS) as well as alternatives using HTML itself. The route will steer you clear of most of the problems caused by differences between different brands and versions of browsers.

For style sheets to work, it is important that your markup be free of errors. A convenient way to automatically fix markup errors is to use the HTML Tidy utility. This also tidies the markup making it easier to read and easier to edit. I recommend you regularly run Tidy over any markup you are editing. Tidy is very effective at cleaning up markup created by authoring tools with sloppy habits.

The following will teach you how to:

- Use the style element
- Link to separate style sheets
- Set page margins
- Set left and right and first-line indents
- Set the amount of whitespace above and below
- Set the font type, style and size

- Add borders and backgrounds
- Set colours with named or numeric values
- Add style for browsers that don't understand CSS

Getting Started

Let's start with setting the colour of the text and the background. You can do this by using the STYLE element to set style properties for the document's tags:

```
<style type="text/css">
 body {colour: black; background: white;}
</style>
```

The style element is placed within the document head. Here is a template HTML file showing where the above style element fits. You can copy and paste this into your editor as a convenient way to experiment with CSS style sheets:

```
<!DOCTYPE html PUBLIC"-//W3C//DTD HTML 4.01 Transitional//EN"
  "http://www.w3.org/TR/html4/loose.dtd">
<html>
<head>
<title> replace with your document's title </title>
<style type="text/css">
 body {colour: black; background: white;}
</style>
</head>
<body>
replace with your document's content
</body>
</html>
```

The stuff between the <style> and </style> is written in special notation for style rules. Each rule starts with a tag name followed by a list of style properties bracketed by {and}. In this example, the rule matches the body tag. As you will see, the body tag provides the basis for setting the overall look and feel of your Web page.

Each style property starts with the property's name, then a colon and lastly the value for this property. When there is more than one style property in the list, you need to use a semicolon between each of them to delimit one property from the next. In this example, there are two properties–"colour" which sets the colour of the text, and"background" which sets the colour of the page background. I recommend always adding the semicolon even after the last property.

Colours can be given as names or as numerical values, for instance rgb(255, 204, 204) which is a fleshy pink. The 3 numbers correspond to red, green and blue respectively in the range 0 to 255.

You can also use a hexadecimal notation, the same colour can also be written as #FFCCCC. More details on colour are given in a later section.

Note that the style element must be placed in the document's head along with the title element. It shouldn't be placed within the body.

Linking to a Separate Style Sheet

If you are likely to want to use the same styles for several Web pages it is worth considering using a separate style sheet which you then link from each page. You can do this as follows:

```
<link type="text/css" rel="stylesheet"
href="style.css">
```

The link tag should be placed within the <head>... </head> element. Here is an HTML file with a link to an external style sheet:

```
<!DOCTYPE html PUBLIC"-//W3C//DTD HTML 4.01
Transitional//EN"
   "http://www.w3.org/TR/html4/loose.dtd">
<html>
<head>
<title> replace with your document's title </
title>
<link type="text/css" rel="stylesheet"
href="style.css">
</head>
<body>
replace with your document's content
```

```
</body>
</html>
```

Setting the Page Margins

Web pages look a lot nicer with bigger margins. You can set the left and right margins with the"margin-left" and"margin-right" properties, *e.g.*

```
<style type="text/css">
 body {margin-left: 10%; margin-right: 10%;}
</style>
```

This sets both margins to 10% of the window width, and the margins will scale when you resize the browser window.

Setting left and right indents

To make headings a little more distinctive, you can make them start within the margin set for the body, *e.g.*

```
<style type="text/css">
 body {margin-left: 10%; margin-right: 10%;}
 h1 {margin-left: -8%;}
 h2,h3,h4,h5,h6 {margin-left: -4%;}
</style>
```

This example has three style rules. One for the body, one for h1 (used for the most important headings) and one for the rest of the headings (h2, h3, h4, h5 and h6).The margins for the headings are additive to the margins for the body. Negative values are used to move the start of the headings to the left of the margin set for the body. In the following sections, the examples of particular style rules will need to be placed within the style element in the document's head or in a linked style sheet.

Controlling the White Space Above and Below

Browsers do a pretty good job for the white space above and below headings and paragraphs etc. Two reasons for taking control of this yourself are: when you want a lot of white space before a particular heading or paragraph, or when you need precise control for the general spacings.

The"margin-top" property specifies the space above and the"margin-bottom" specifies the space below. To set these for all h2 headings you can write:

```
h2 {margin-top: 8em; margin-bottom: 3em;}
```

The em is a very useful unit as it scales with the size of the font. One em is the height of the font. By using em's you can preserve the general look of the Web page independently of the font size. This is much safer than alternatives such as pixels or points, which can cause problems for users who need large fonts to read the text.

Points are commonly used in word processing packages, *e.g.* 10pt text. Unfortunately the same point size is rendered differently on different browsers. What works fine for one browser will be illegible on another! Sticking with em's avoids these problems.

To specify the space above a particular heading, you should create a named style for the heading. You do this with the class attribute in the markup, *e.g.*

```
<h2 class="subsection">Getting started</h2>
```

The Style Rule is then Written as

```
h2.subsection {margin-top: 8em; margin-bottom:
3em;}
```

The rule starts with the tag name, a dot and then the value of the class attribute. Be careful to avoid placing a space before or after the dot. If you do the rule won't work. There are other ways to set the styles for a particular element but the class attribute is the most flexible.

When a heading is followed by a paragraph, the value for margin-bottom for the heading isn't added to the value for margin-top for the paragraph. Instead, the maximum of the two values is used for the spacing between the heading and paragraph. This subtlety applies to margin-top and margin-bottom regardless of which tags are involved.

First-line Indent

Sometimes you may want to indent the first line of each paragraph. The following style rule emulates the traditional way paragraphs are rendered in novels:

```
p {text-indent: 2em; margin-top: 0; margin-bottom:
0;}
```

It indents the first line of each paragraph by 2 em's and suppresses the inter-paragraph spacing.

Controlling the font

This section explains how to set the font and size, and how to add italic, bold and other styles.

Font styles: The most common styles are to place text in italic or bold. Most browsers render the em tag in italic and thestrong tag in bold. Let's assume you instead want em to appear in bold italic and strong in bold uppercase:

```
em {font-style: italic; font-weight: bold;}
strong {text-transform: uppercase; font-weight:
bold;}
```

If you feel so inclined, you can fold headings to lower case as follows:

```
h2 {text-transform: lowercase;}
```

Setting the Font Size

Most browsers use a larger font size for more important headings. If you override the default size, you run the risk of making the text too small to be legible, particularly if you use points. You are therefore recommended to specify font sizes in relative terms.

This example sets heading sizes in percentages relative to the size used for normal text:

```
h1 {font-size: 200%;}
h2 {font-size: 150%;}
h3 {font-size: 100%;}
```

Setting the Font Family

It is likely that your favourite font won't be available on all browsers. To get around this, you are allowed to list several fonts in preference order.

There is a short list of generic font names which are guaranteed to be available, so you are recommended to end your list with one of these: serif, sans-serif, cursive, fantasy, or monospace, for instance:

```
body {font-family: Verdana, sans-serif;}
```

```
h1,h2 {font-family: Garamond,"Times New Roman",
serif;}
```

In this example, important headings would preferably be shown in Garamond, failing that in Times New Roman, and if that is unavailable in the browsers default serif font. Paragraph text would appear in Verdana or if that is unavailable in the browser's default sans-serif font. The legibility of different fonts generally depends more on the height of lower case letters than on the font size itself. Fonts like Verdana are much more legible than ones like"Times New Roman" and are therefore recommended for paragraph text.

Avoid Problems with Fonts and Margins

My first rule is to avoid text at the body level that isn't wrapped in a block level element such as p. For instance:

```
<h2>Spring in Wiltshire</h2>
```

Blossom on the trees, bird song and the sound of lambs bleating in the fields. The text following the heading runs the risk on some browsers of being rendered with the wrong font and margins. You are therefore advised to enclose all such text in a paragraph, *e.g.*

```
<h2>Spring in Wiltshire</h2>
<p>Blossom on the trees, bird song and the sound
of lambs
bleating in the fields.</p>
```

My second rule is to set the font family for pre elements, as some browsers forget to use a fixed pitch font when you set the font size or other properties for pre.

```
pre {font-family: monospace;}
```

My third rule is to set the font family on headings, p and ul elements if you intend to set borders or backgrounds on elements such as div. This is a work-around for a bug where the browser forgets to use the inherited font family, instead switching to the default font as set by the browser preferences.

h1,h2,h3,h4,h5,p,ul {font-family: sans-serif;}

Adding Borders and Backgrounds

You can easily add a border around a heading, list,

paragraph or a group of these enclosed with a div element. For instance:

```
div.box {border: solid; border-width: thin; width:
100%;}
```

Note that without the"width" property some browsers will place the right margin too far to the right. This can then be used with markup such as:

```
<div class="box">
    The content within this DIV element will be enclosed
    in a box with a thin line around it.
</div>
```

There are a limited choice of border types: dotted, dashed, solid, double, groove, ridge, inset and outset. The border-width property sets the width. Its values include thin, medium and thick as well as a specified width *e.g.* 0.1em. The border-colour property allows you to set the colour.

Setting Colours

Some examples for setting colours appeared in earlier sections. Here is a reminder:

```
body {
colour: black;
background: white;
}
strong {colour: red;}
```

This sets the default to black text on a white background, but renders strong elements in red. There are 16 standard colour name, which are explained just below. You can also use decimal values for red, green and blue, where each value appears in the range 0 to 255, *e.g.* rgb(255, 0, 0) is the same as red. You can also used hex colour values which start with the'#' characted followed by six hexadecimal digits. A two-way converter is included below which allows you to convert from RGB to hex colour values.

Setting Link Colours

You can use CSS to set the colour for hypertext links, with a different colour for links that you have yet to follow, ones you have followed, and the active colour for when the link is being clicked. You can even set the colour for when the mouse pointer is hovering over the link.

```
:link {colour: rgb(0, 0, 153);}/* for unvisited
links */
:visited {colour: rgb(153, 0, 153);}/* for visited
links */
a:active {colour: rgb(255, 0, 102);}/* when link
is clicked */
a:hover {colour: rgb(0, 96, 255);}/* when mouse
is over link */
```

Sometimes you may want to show hypertext links without them being underlined. You can do this by setting thetext-decoration property to none, for example:

```
a.plain {text-decoration: none;}
```

Which would suppress underlining for a link such as:

```
This is <a class="plain" href="what.html">not
underlined</a>
```

Most people when they see underlined text on a Web page, will expect it to be part of a hypertext link. As a result, you are advised to leave underlining on for hypertext links. A similar argument applies to the link colours, most people will interpret underlined blue text as hypertext links. You are advised to leave link colours alone, except when the colour of the background would otherwise make the text hard to read.

Colour Blindness

When using colour, remember that 5 to 10% of men have some form of colour blindness. This can cause difficulties distinguishing between red and green, or between yellow and blue. In rare cases, there is an inability to perceive any colours at all. You are recommended to avoid foreground/background colour combinations that would make the text hard to read for people with colour blindness.

What About Browsers that don't Support CSS

Older browsers, that is to say before Netscape 4.0 and Internet Explorer 4.0, either don't support CSS at all or do so inconsistently. For these browsers you can still control the style by using HTML itself.

Setting the Colour and Background

You can set the colour using the BODY tag. The following example sets the background colour to white and the text colour to black:

```
<body bgcolour="white" text="black">
```

The BODY element should be placed before the visible content of the Web page, *e.g.* before the first heading. You can also control the colour of hypertext links.

There are three attributes for this:

- Link for unvisited links
- Vlink for visited links
- Alink for the colour used when you click the link

Here is an example that sets all three:

```
<body bgcolour="white" text="black"
link="navy" vlink="maroon" alink="red">
```

You can also get the browser to tile the page background with an image using the background attribute to specify the Web address for the image, *e.g.*

```
<body bgcolour="white" background="texture.jpeg"
text="black"
link="navy" vlink="maroon" alink="red">
```

It is a good idea to specify a background colour using the bgcolour attribute in case the browser is unable to render the image. You should check that the colours you have chosen don't cause legibility problems. As an extreme case consider the following:

```
<body bgcolour="black">
```

Most browsers will render text in black by default. The end result is that the page will be shown with black text on a black background! Lots of people suffer from one form of colour blindness or another, for example olive green may appear brown to some people.

A separate problem appears when you try to print the Web page. Many browsers will ignore the background colour, but will obey the text colour. Setting the text to white will often result in a blank page when printed, so the following is not recommended:

```
<body bgcolour="black" text="white">
```

You can also use the bgcolour attribute on table cells, *e.g.*

```
<table border="0" cellpadding="5">
<tr>
<td bgcolour="yellow">coloured table cell</td>
</tr>
</table>
```

Tables can be used for a variety of layout effects and have been widely exploited for this. In the future this role is likely to be supplanted by style sheets, which make it practical to achieve precise layout with less effort.

Getting Further Information

For further information on CSS and tools that support it, you should look at the W3C home page for CSS. This includes pointers to books on HTML and CSS, for example,"Raggett on HTML 4", published 1998 by Addison Wesley. For a more detailed explanation of CSS,"Cascading Style Sheets" by Håkon Wium Lie and Bert Bos, pub. 2005 by Addison Wesley, which provides an in-depth look at CSS as seen by the architects of CSS themselves. Some errata are also available for this book.

3

HTML Versions

1992 HTML IS FIRST DEFINED

The WWW system uses marked-up text to represent a hypertext document for transmision over the network. The hypertext mark-up language is an SGMLformat. WWW parsers should ignore tags which they do not understand, and ignore attributes which they do not understand of tags which they do understand.

To find out how to write HTML, or to write a programme to generate it, read the following sections:

- *Default text*: How text is interpreted when uninfluenced by tags
- *The tags*: A list of the tags used in HTML with their significance.
- *Entities*: Special characters are represented by SGML entities

DTD: The SGML document type definition for HTML.

The following do not form part of the specifciation.

Example:

- A file containing a variety of tags used for test purposes. See also finding examples on the web.
- *Future directions*: Changes suggested for HTML improvements
- *Constraints*: Design constraints for HTML which might explain some of its properties.

1993 HTML+ (SOME PHYSICAL LAYOUT, FILL-OUT FORMS, TABLES, MATH)

HTML+ is a set of modular extensions to the hypertext

markup language (HTML), which is in widespread use in the World Wide Web. The use of SGML to specify HTML+ allows authors to create documents in a variety of ways: with text editors, SGML authoring tools and filters from common word processing formats like Fram- emaker, Microsoft Word and LaTeX.

The paper finishes by looking at extensions under current consideration and encouraging wider debate on what is needed to fuel the next stage in the development of the Web.

INTRODUCTION

In 1450 Johannes Gutenberg is credited with bringing together two ideas: the use of metal dies to make moveable type and a press for obtaining sharp impressions on sheets of paper. The invention of printing at the dawn of the age of great discoveries accelerated economic, social and ideological changes that were to usher in the modern world.

Traditional media like books, newspapers, radio, cinema and television are published by the few for the many, while telephones are limited to one to one conversations. The World Wide Web is a radically new media, bringing together hypertext, logical markup and global networking.

The Web makes it very easy for anyone to publish information to people located anywhere in the world. The Web is growing at a very rapid rate–doubling in traffic every two to three months. At the time of writing some 400 Gigabytes was being carried per month.

There is now a great body of experience in laying out the printed word. That experience brings with it a fixation with the printed page. The development of computers has perpetuated that fixation: Word processing software has been seen principally as a means of preparing printed documents. Global networks now make it easy to distribute information electronically and the time has come to shake off the limitations of the printed page.

Today, many of the formats for electronic distribution of information embody the restrictions of the printed page– documents are broken into a sequence of fixed sized pages and pages are described in terms of marks to be made at specified positions, usually involving named fonts. This has prevented true interchangeability of information. Many of you will have seen this with Postscript–for some reason or other a problem often occurs when trying to print out that paper you just retrieved over the net!

The Standard Generalized Markup Language (SGML) was invented as a solution to these problems. By focussing on the logical elements in a document, the recipient of information is freed from the often inappropriate choices of the originator. Users can resize their windows to make optimal use of their screens and printing software can layout documents to match local paper sizes.

Other benefits from using SGML include the ability to protect the investment of information providers in the face of short lived proprietary formats, and the availability of tools for authoring and format conversion.

SGML is a metaformat that allows one to specify a wide range of document formats. The hypertext markup language HTML was developed as a simple non-proprietary delivery format for global hypertext. HTML+ is a set of modular extensions to HTML and has been developed in response to a growing understanding of the needs of information providers. These extensions include text flow around floating figures, fill-out forms, tables and mathematical equations.

Browsers are programmes for viewing HTML documents and are now available for most platforms. The best known are the Mosaic family of browsers from the U.S. National Center for Supercomputing Applications, with browsers for X11, Windows, and the Macintosh.

Non-graphical browsers are available for VT100 terminals etc, for example Lynx and Emacs-W3. The appearence of a document will vary from one browser to the next according to the capabilities of each system and the user's preferences. Currently, most documents are created with conventional text editors.

The effort needed to type the markup elements can be reduced by using post-processing tools to ensure that the resulting document complies with the HTML document type definition (DTD). Authors can also use common word processing packages and apply filters to convert to HTML. Filters are available for FrameMaker, LaTeX and Microsoft Word. Other people are using standard SGML tools for document authoring and conversion from proprietary SGML based document formats.

AN OVERVIEW OF HTML

HTML includes markup elements for:

- Headers
- Paragraphs
- Various types of character highlighting
- Character-like in-line images
- Hypertext links
- Lists
- Preformatted text
- Simple search facility

Here is a simple example of an HTML document:

```
<title>A sample HTML document</title>
<h1>An example of Structure</h1>
Here's a typical <i>paragraph</i><p>
<ul>
  <li>Item one has an <a name="anchor">anchor</
     a>
  <li>The next item has a <a
    href="link.html">hypertext link</a>.
  </ul>
```

The TITLE element is used to name the document as a whole. There are six levels of headers of decreasing importance ranging from H1 to H6. The P element indicates a paragraph break. HTML supports four styles of character highlighting: fixed-width teletype font TT, bold face B, italic I and underlined U. Browsers can choose to render them in alternative ways or even to ignore them altogether. There are in addition several logical styles.

Hypertext links are represented with the anchor tag, and restricted to unidirectional binary links. The text between the start tag <a> and the end tag </a> is used as the caption. Links are usually made to a document as a whole but can also be made to anchors within a document. The example shows an anchor being used with the NAME attribute to declare a potential destination for such a link. The HREF attribute is used to identify the linked document via a universal resource locator (URL). This is a naming scheme for referencing objects located anywhere in the network.

URLs start with a prefix that describe the access method or protocol for retrieving the referenced object, and is usually followed by an Internet host name and path. Relative references provide a convenient method of abbreviating URLs and are expanded in the context of the full URL for the current document. A reference to the specification of URLs can be found in section 5 at the end of this document.

There are several kinds of lists: definition lists DL, ordered (numbered) lists OL, bulleted lists UL and plain lists (MENU and DIR). Lists cannot be nested, although in practice, most browsers relax this restriction. Preformatted text is represented with the PRE tag, and can include character highlighting and hypertext links. It was introduced to make it easy to import the output of existing computer programmes, *e.g.* Unix manual pages. HTML includes a simple search facility (the <ISINDEX> tag) where users can type in a string of characters and send them to a server for interpretation.

The HEAD and BODY elements can be used to separate the front matter from the document body. The document's head is used for information pertaining to the document as a whole, such as the title, whether it supports searches: ISINDEX, and relationships with other documents, expressed with the LINK element.

A Comparison Between HTML+ and HTML

HTML+ adds new features like figures, tables and forms. It also generalizes the structures present in HTML to reflect practical experience with writing browsers and a desire to make it easier to convert between HTML+ and other formats. These changes are reviewed below before presenting major new features. This part of the paper assumes some prior familiarization with the HTML document format.

Most browsers now support nested lists. HTML+ formalizes this, allowing arbitrary nesting of the various kinds of lists. Lists items can now include the horizontal rule element HR. A further extension under consideration is to allow preformatted text in list items using the PRE element. The DIR and MENU elements have been replaced by a more powerful version of the UL element for unordered lists. The PLAIN attribute suppresses bullets, while the WRAP attribute specifies the wrap style (vertical or horizontal) for multicolumn lists. Bullets can also be replaced by icons, using the SRC attribute to specify a URL for an image.

A number of elements have been made into containers. These include paragraphs P, list items LI, DT and DD. This change has little effect on authors, but helps with document conversion, and brings HTML into accord with other SGML formats. It also makes it practical to associate attributes with the contained text, *e.g.* character sets and paragraph alignment. Most elements now accept an ID attribute, which provides a name unique within that document, and can be used as the destination of hypertext links. This is a common technique in SGML documents. The new charset attribute can be used to specify the character set on an element by element basis, *e.g.* ISO-2022-JP for japanese.

Strike through S, is a new style for character highlighting and particularly useful for legal documents. Highlighting elements can now be nested, *e.g.* for bold-italic text. Other innovations include subscripts SUB and superscripts SUP, in-line quotes Q, and support for change bars changed. The element for longer quotes has been abbreviated to quote. A forced line break is now possible with the BR element. LaTeX style tab stops can be defined with the TAB element. The range of character entities has been considerably expanded to cover a wide range of symbols, for example: for a non-breaking space and © for a copyright sign. Entity names are also defined for standard icons for use as annotations in directory listings, *e.g.* &folder; and other applications.

Character-like images are supported using the existing IMG element. The ALT attribute can be used to give a textual description for non-graphical browsers. The vertical position of the image relative to the baseline can be specified as before with the align attribute (top, middle or bottom), but greater precision is possible with the new baseline attribute which adjusts the image so that the baseline occurs at the specified number of pixels above the bottom of the image. The ISMAP attribute allows users to pass clicks on the image through to the server as an offset from the top-left corner of the image. This is useful for graphical menus or active maps.

Some New Elements

The footnote element is intended for additional information and can be implemented as an internal jump to the end of the document or as a pop-up panel. The margin element is useful for attracting people's attention with a snappy phrase placed in the margin or rendered as a separate paragraph in a largish font, perhaps marked off by horizontal rules. The abstract element is used as its name gests, typically being placed just after a major heading. The note element is used for admonishments. The role attribute is one of simple, tip, note, warning or error. This element is usually rendered with an icon in the left margin according to the role attribute with the text inset accordingly. The default icons are typically: none for simple, an upright hand with an outstretched finger for tip, an information sign for note, a traffic warning sign for warning and a stop sign for error. These icons can be overridden by using the SRC attribute to specify a URL for the image.

Tables

Tables are specified using the table element. This allows you to define a caption (above or below the table) and to differentiate header and data cells. Cells may contain, text, images, multiple paragraphs, lists and headers. Adjacent cells can be merged, *e.g.* to define a header which spans two columns. A simple table could look like:

Each row is contained within a TR element, although the end tag may be omitted. The border attribute acts as a hint to the browser to draw lines enclosing each cell. The TH element precedes header cell text and the TD element precedes data cell text. By default text is centered in each cell. Header text should be shown emphasized, *e.g.* the browser could use a bold sans serif font for headers and a serif font for the data cells. The next example shows how cells can be merged with their neighbours:

Hypertext Paths

Authors can create guided tours through the web. These are defined using HTML+ documents in which links specify a sequence of documents to present to the user. The NODE attribute in the anchor element is used to signify that a particular link should form part of the path, *e.g.*

```
<P>This is a sample path:
<UL>
     <LI><P>This is the <A HREF=node1.html"
        NODE>first node
     <LI><P>and this is the <A HREF=node2.html"
        NODE>second node
</UL>
```

You can compose paths by using the PATH attribute to indicate that a link references another path, *e.g.*

```
<A HREF="path.html" PATH>inserts the linked path
   into the current one</A>
```

Users can move along a path via next and previous buttons on the browser's toolbar (or navigation menu). Additional buttons can be defined using the LINK element to specify links to the table of contents and author defined bookmarks. The specification allows for LINK elements to be dynamically added to documents via the HTTP protocol. This is used by the path mechanism to imply link elements for the active path, and previous/next nodes in that path. These richer navigation mechanisms are intended to reduce the chances that users will feel"lost in hyperspace" when browsing through complex material.

Where Next

Most browsers now support simple fill-out forms, following the pioneering work by NCSA on X Mosaic. Support for tables and figures is currently thin on the ground. Viola provides limited support for tables and NCSA are working on adding these features to Mosaic. The author's X11 HTML+ browser should help to speed up this process. The Internet Draft for HTML+ lapsed at the beginning of May, and is being replaced, and is now available in hypertext form via the Web.

Information providers are interested in making their documents appear in a particular style which differentiates them from other information providers. Work is under way to see how HTML+ could support style information without limiting platform independence. Style hints could be expressed as part of the document head and cover aspects such as font families, text colour and size, and the use of whitespace around elements.

The use of images, and the opportunity to set the colour and texture of the background offer further ways of creating a unique style. Another idea is to define a document specific toolbar using LINK elements. Custom images for links will be possible using the SRC attribute. In-line images are currently limited to the GIF format. A natural extension will be to support JPEG and even MPEG.

The Web is also missing the capability to compose images from multiple sources. It would be desirable to be able to overlay line graphics on top of bitmapped images or say a small video inset on a static image. Much work remains to be done on how to compose and coordinate multimedia sources. The ISO HyTime standard is likely to be of relevance to this work.

The possibilities for extending the World Wide Web to include virtual reality are being covered in another paper in this conference. The author is also involved with work on adapting the World Wide Web to work on ATM networks, which offer dramatic improvements in speed over current network technologies, and rich opportunities for novel multimedia applications, for example integration with the telephone service for voice mail, and video-telephone calls. The Web looks like providing an excellent way for users to browse through multicast"radio" and"television" channels. HTML+ is expected to play an important role as the hypertext glue that bridges the gaps between such services, *e.g.* by providing a means for users to browse through what's-on guides and follow links to particular channels or videos-on-demand.

The development of commercial services using the web will be greatly stimulated by global deployment of public key cryptography. The waiving of licence fees for freeware implementations of browsers and servers is expected to speed widespread adoption of these technique.

The development of effective directory services is also going to play an increasingly important role. The deployment of commercial services will in turn provide the resources to develop improved browsers and document conversion tools, and feed through into the continuing evolution of hypermedia document formats.

1994 HTML 2.0 (STANDARD FOR CORE FEATURES)

The HTML 2.0 specification RFC 1866, is a product of the HTML Working Group of the IETF, edited by Dan Connolly.

RFC 1866. PROPOSED STANDARD

"HyperText Markup Language Specification -- 2.0",
T. Berners-Lee and D. Connolly, November 1995.

The Hypertext Markup Language (HTML) is a simple markup language used to create hypertext documents that are platform independent. HTML documents are SGML documents with generic semantics that are appropriate for representing information from a wide range of domains. HTML markup can represent hypertext news, mail, documentation, and hypermedia; menus of options; database query results; simple structured documents with in-lined graphics; and hypertext views of existing bodies of information.

HTML has been in use by the World Wide Web (WWW) global information initiative since 1990. This specification roughly corresponds to the capabilities of HTML in common use prior to June 1994. HTML is an application of ISO Standard 8879:1986 Information Processing Text and Office Systems; Standard Generalized Markup Language (SGML).

INTRODUCTION

HyperText Markup Language (HTML) is a simple markup system used to create hypertext documents that are portable from one platform to another. HTML documents are SGML documents with generic semantics that are appropriate for representing information from a wide range of applications. HTML markup can represent hypertext news, mail, documentation, and hypermedia; menus of options; database query results; simple structured documents with in-lined graphics; and hypertext views of existing bodies of information.

HTML has been in use by the World-Wide Web (WWW) global information initiative since 1990. The HTML 3.0 specification provides a number of new features, and is broadly backwards compatible with HTML 2.0.

It is defined as an application of International Standard ISO ISO8879:1986 Standard Generalized Markup Language (SGML). This specificiation will be proposed as the Internet Media Type (RFC 1590) and MIME Content Type (RFC 1521) called"text/html; version=3.0".

HTML 3.0

The process of refining HTML 3.0 into a formal standard will be carried out by the IETF HTML working group. The World Wide Web Organization is continuing to develop a freeware testbed browser for HTML 3.0 ("Arena") to encourage people to try out the proposed features.

The discussion list for HTML 3.0 is www-html with html-wg reserved for use by the IETF working group for detailed matters relating to the formal specification. The process for developing HTML 3.0 is open, and anyone who is interested and able to contribute to this effort is welcome to join in.

Transition Strategy from HTML 2.0

The use of the MIME content type:"text/html; version=3.0"

is recommended to prevent existing HTML 2.0 user agents screwing up by attempting to show 3.0 documents. Tests have shown that the suggested content type will safely cause existing user agents to display the save to file dialog rather than incorrectly displaying the document as if it were HTML 2.0.

To make it easy for servers to distinguish 3.0 documents from 2.0 documents, it is suggested that 3.0 files are saved with the extension".html3" (or".ht3" for PCs). Servers can also exploit the accept headers in HTTP requests from HTML user agents, to distinguish whether each client can or cannot support HTML 3.0. This makes it practical for information providers to start providing HTML 3.0 versions of existing documents for newer user agents, without impacting older user agents. It is envisaged that programmes will be made available for automatic down conversion of 3.0 to 2.0 documents. This conversion could be carried out in batch mode, or on the fly (with caching for greater efficiency).

Design Guidelines

The HTML 3.0 draft specification has been written to the following guidelines.

Lingua Franca for the Web: HTML is intended as a common medium for tying together information from widely different sources. A means to rise above the interoperability problems with existing document formats, and a means to provide a truly open interface to proprietary information systems.

Simplicity

The first version of HTML was designed to be extremely simple, both to author and to write browsers for. This has played a major role in the incredibly rapid growth of the World Wide Web. HTML 3.0 provides a clean superset of HTML 2.0 adding high value features such as tables, text flow around figures and math, while still remaining a simple document format. The pressures to adopt the complexities of traditional SGML applications has been resisted, for example the Department of Defence's CALS table model or the ISO 12083 math DTD.

Scaleability

As time goes by, people's expectations change, and more will be demanded of HTML. One manifestation of this is the pressure to add yet more tags. HTML 3.0 introduces a means for subclassing elements in an open-ended way.

This can be used to distinguish the role of a paragraph element as being a couplet in a stansa, or a mathematical term as being a tensor. This ability to make fresh distinctions can be exploited to impart distinct rendering styles or to support richer search mechanisms, without further complicating the HTML document format itself. Scaleability is also achieved via URI based links for embedding information in other formats. Initially limited to a few image formats, inline support is expected to rapidly evolve to cover drawing formats, video, distributed virtual reality and a general means for embedding other applications.

Platform Independence

HTML is designed to allow rendering on a very wide range of devices, from clunky teletypes, to terminals, DOS, Windows, Macs and high end Workstations, as well as non-visual media such as speech and braille. In this, it allows users to exploit the legacy of older equipment as well as the latest and best of new machines. HTML 3.0 provides for improved support for non-graphical clients, allowing for rich markup in place of the figures shown on graphical clients. HTML can be rendered on a wide variety of screen sizes, using a scrolling or paged model. The fonts and presentation can be adjusted to suit the resources available in the host machine and the user's preferences.

Content not Presentation Markup

Information providers are used to tight control over the final appearence of documents. The need for platform independence weighs against this, but there is still a strong pressure to find appropriate means for information providers to express their intentions. The experience with proprietary document formats has shown the dangers of mixing presentation markup with content (or structural) markup. It becomes difficult to apply different presentation styles. It becomes painful to incorporate material from different sources (with different presentation styles). It becomes difficult to be truly platform independent. As a result, HTML 3.0 is designed for use with linked style information that defines the intended presentation style for each element. Style sheets can be expressed in a platform independent fashion or used to provide more detailed control for particular classes of clients or output media.

Support for Cascaded Style Sheets

For the Web, it is valuable to allow for a cascading of style preferences. The client has certain built-in preferences; the publisher may require a particular house style, *e.g.* for brand distinction; the author may feel the need to override the house style for special cases; the end-user may feel strongly about certain things, *e.g.*

large fonts for easier visibility or avoiding certain colours due to an inability to distinguish between them. HTML 3.0 supports style sheets via the use of the LINK element to reference a style sheet with a URI. Authors can place overrides in separate style sheets or include them in the document head within the STYLE element. The effectiveness of caching mechanisms for speeding up the retrieval of style sheets is enhanced by the separation of style information into generic commonly used style sheets, and overrides specific to this document.

Support for Non-Visual Media

HTML 3.0 is designed to cater for the needs of the visually impaired. Markup for inline figures includes support for rich descriptions, along with hypertext links that double up as defining geometric hotzones for graphical browsers, simplifying the author's job in catering for the different groups of users. Table markup includes provision for abbreviated row and column names for each cell, which are essential for conversion to speech or braille. Math markup treats formulae and equations as hierarchies of expressions. This allows disambiguating pauses to be inserted in appropriate places during conversion to speech.

Support for Different ways of Creating HTML

HTML 3.0 has been designed to be created in a variety of different ways. It is deliberately simple enough to type in by hand. It can be authored using wysiwyg editors for HTML, or it can be generated via export filters from common word processing formats, or other SGML applications.

INTRODUCTION TO HTML 3.2

HTML 3.2 is W3C's specification for HTML, developed in early `96 together with vendors including IBM, Microsoft, Netscape Communications Corporation, Novell, SoftQuad, Spyglass, and Sun Microsystems.

HTML 3.2 adds widely deployed features such as tables, applets and text flow around images, while providing full backwards compatibility with the existing standard HTML 2.0.

W3C is continuing to work with vendors on extensions for accessibility features, multimedia objects, scripting, style sheets, layout, forms, math and internationalization. W3C plans on incorporating this work in further versions of HTML.

HTML as an SGML Application

HTML 3.2 is an SGML application conforming to International Standard ISO 8879 -- Standard Generalized Markup Language. As an SGML application, the syntax of conforming HTML 3.2 documents is defined by the combination of the SGML declaration and the document type definition (DTD).

This specification defines the intended interpretation of HTML 3.2 elements, and places further constraints on the permitted syntax which are otherwise inexpressible in the DTD.

The SGML rules for record boundaries are tricky. In particular, a record end immediately following a start tag should be discarded.

For example:

```
<P>
Text
```

is equivalent to:

```
<P>Text
```

Similarly, a record end immediately preceding an end tag should be discarded. For example:

```
Text
</P>
```

is equivalent to:

```
Text</P>
```

Except within literal text (*e.g.* the PRE element), HTML treats contiguous sequences of white space characters as being equivalent to a single space character (ASCII decimal 32). These rules allow authors considerable flexibility when editing the marked-up text directly. Note that future revisions to HTML may allow for the interpretation of the horizontal tab character (ASCII decimal 9) with respect to a tab rule defined by an associated style sheet.

SGML entities in PCDATA content or in CDATA attributes are expanded by the parser, *e.g.* é is expanded to the ISO Latin-1 character decimal 233 (a lower case letter e with an acute accent). This could also have been written as a named character entity, *e.g.* é. The and character can be included in its own right using the named character entity &.

HTML allows CDATA attributes to be unquoted provided the attribute value contains only letters (a to z and A to Z), digits (0 to 9), hyphens (ASCII decimal 45) or, periods (ASCII decimal 46). Attribute values can be quoted using double or single quote marks (ASCII decimal 34 and 39 respectively). Single quote marks can be included within the attribute value when the value is delimited by double quote marks, and vice versa.

Note that some user agents require attribute minimisation for the following attributes: COMPACT, ISMAP, CHECKED, NOWRAP, NOSHADE and NOHREF. These user agents don't accept syntax such as COMPACT=COMPACT or

ISMAP=ISMAP although this is legitimate according to the HTML 3.2 DTD.

The SGML declaration and the DTD for use with HTML 3.2 are given in appendices. Further guidelines for parsing HTML are given in WD-html-lex.

The Structure of HTML documents

HTML 3.2 Documents start with a <!DOCTYPE> declaration followed by an HTML element containing a HEAD and then a BODY element:

```
<!DOCTYPE HTML PUBLIC"-//W3C//DTD HTML 3.2 Final/
/EN">
<HTML>
<HEAD>
<TITLE>A study of population dynamics</TITLE>
... other head elements
</HEAD>
<BODY>
... document body
</BODY>
</HTML>
```

In practice, the HTML, HEAD and BODY start and end tags can be omitted from the markup as these can be inferred in all cases by parsers conforming to the HTML 3.2 DTD.

Every conforming HTML 3.2 document must start with the <!DOCTYPE> declaration that is needed to distinguish HTML 3.2 documents from other versions of HTML. The HTML specification is not concerned with storage entities. As a result, it is not required that the document type declaration reside in the same storage entity (*i.e.* file). A Web site may choose to dynamically prepend HTML files with the document type declaration if it is known that all such HTML files conform to the HTML 3.2 specification.

Every HTML 3.2 document must also include the descriptive title element. A minimal HTML 3.2 document thus looks like:

```
<!DOCTYPE HTML PUBLIC"-//W3C//DTD HTML 3.2 Final/
/EN">
```

```
<TITLE>A study of population dynamics</TITLE>
```

Note: the word"Final" replaces"Draft" now that the HTML 3.2 specification has been ratified by the W3C member organizations.

THE HEAD ELEMENT

This contains the document head, but you can always omit both the start and end tags for HEAD.

The contents of the document head is an unordered collection of the following elements:

- The TITLE element
- The STYLE element
- The SCRIPT element
- The ISINDEX element
- The BASE element
- The META element
- The LINK element

```
<!ENTITY% head.content"TITLE and ISINDEX? and
BASE?">
<!ENTITY% head.misc"SCRIPT|STYLE|META|LINK">
<!ELEMENT HEAD O O (%head.content) +(%head.misc)>
```

The%head.misc entity is used to allow the associated elements to occur multiple times at arbitrary positions within the HEAD.

The following elements can be part of the document head:

- Title defines the document title, and is always needed.
- ISINDEX for simple keyword searches, see PROMPT attribute.
- Base defines base URL for resolving relative URLs.
- Script reserved for future use with scripting languages.
- Style reserved for future use with style sheets.
- Mrta used to supply meta info as name/value pairs.
- Link used to define relationships with other documents.
- Title, Script and Style are containers and require both start and end tags. The other elements are not

containers so that end tags are forbidden. Note that conforming browsers won't render the contents of Script and Style elements.

TITLE

```
<!ELEMENT TITLE-- (#PCDATA)* -(%head.misc)>
```

Every HTML 3.2 document must have exactly one TITLE element in the document's HEAD. It provides an advisory title which can be displayed in a user agent's window caption etc. The content model is PCDATA.

As a result, character entities can be used for accented characters and to escape special characters such as & and <. Markup is not permitted in the content of a TITLE element.

Example TITLE element:

```
<TITLE>A study of population dynamics</TITLE>
```

STYLE and SCRIPT

```
<!ELEMENT STYLE-- CDATA -- placeholder for style
info -->
<!ELEMENT SCRIPT-- CDATA -- placeholder for script
statements -->
```

These are place holders for the introduction of style sheets and client-side scripts in future versions of HTML. User agents should hide the contents of these elements. These elements are defined with CDATA as the content type. As a result they may contain only SGML characters. All markup characters or delimiters are ignored and passed as data to the application, except for ETAGO ("</") delimiters followed immediately by a name character [a-zA-Z]. This means that the element's end-tag (or that of an element in which it is nested) is recognized, while an error occurs if the ETAGO is invalid.

ISINDEX

```
<!ELEMENT ISINDEX-O EMPTY>
<!ATTLIST ISINDEX
prompt CDATA #IMPLIED -- prompt message -->
```

The ISINDEX element indicates that the user agent should provide a single line text input field for entering a query string. There are no restrictions on the number of characters that can be entered. The PROMPT attribute can be used to specify a prompt string for the input field, *e.g.*

```
<ISINDEX PROMPT="Search Phrase">
```

The semantics for ISINDEX are currently well defined only when the base URL for the enclosing document is an HTTP URL.

Typically, when the user presses the enter (return) key, the query string is sent to the server identified by the base URL for this document. For example, if the query string entered is"ten green apples" and the base URL is:

```
http://www.acme.com/
then the query generated is:
http://www.acme.com/?ten+green+apples"
```

Note that space characters are mapped to"+" characters and that normal URL character escaping mechanisms apply. For further details the HTTP specification.

Note in practice, the query string is resticted to Latin-1 as there is no current mechanism for the URL to specify a character set for the query.

BASE

```
<!ELEMENT BASE-O EMPTY>
<!ATTLIST BASE
href%URL #REQUIRED
>
```

The BASE element gives the base URL for dereferencing relative URLs, using the rules given by the URL specification, *e.g.*

```
<BASE href="http://www.acme.com/intro.html">
...
<IMG SRC="icons/logo.gif">
The image is deferenced to
http://www.acme.com/icons/logo.gif
```

In the absence of a BASE element the document URL should be used. Note that this is not necessarily the same as the URL used to request the document, as the base URL may be overridden by an HTTP header accompanying the document.

META

```
<!ELEMENT META-O EMPTY -- Generic Metainformation
-->
```

```
<!ATTLIST META
http-equiv NAME #IMPLIED -- HTTP response header
name --
name NAME #IMPLIED -- metainformation name --
content CDATA #REQUIRED -- associated information
--
>
```

The META element can be used to include name/value pairs describing properties of the document, such as author, expiry date, a list of key words etc. The NAMEattribute specifies the property name while the CONTENT attribute specifies the property value, *e.g.*

```
<META NAME="Author" CONTENT="Dave Raggett">
```

The HTTP-EQUIV attribute can be used in place of the NAME attribute and has a special significance when documents are retrieved via the Hypertext Transfer Protocol (HTTP).

HTTP servers may use the property name specified by the HTTP-EQUIV attribute to create an RFC 822 style header in the HTTP response.

This can't be used to set certain HTTP headers though, see the HTTP specification for details.

```
<META HTTP-EQUIV="Expires" CONTENT="Tue, 20 Aug
1996 14:25:27 GMT">
```

will result in the HTTP header:

This can be used by caches to determine when to fetch a fresh copy of the associated document.

LINK

LINK provides a media independent method for defining relationships with other documents and resources.

LINK has been part of HTML since the very early days, although few browsers as yet take advantage of it (most still ignore LINK elements).

Link elements can be used in principle:

- For document specific navigation toolbars or menus
- To control how collections of HTML files are rendered into printed documents

- For linking associated resources such as style sheets and scripts
- To provide alternative forms of the current document

```
<!ELEMENT LINK-O EMPTY>
<!ATTLIST LINK
  href%URL #IMPLIED -- URL for linked resource
  --
  rel CDATA #IMPLIED -- forward link types --
  rev CDATA #IMPLIED -- reverse link types --
  title CDATA #IMPLIED -- advisory title string
--
>
```

Href

Specifies a URL designating the linked resource.

Rel

The forward relationship also known as the"link type". It specifies a named relationship from the enclosing document to the resource specified by theHREF attribute. HTML link relationships are as yet unstandardized, although some conventions have been established.

Rev

This defines a reverse relationship. A link from document A to document B with REV=relation expresses the same relationship as a link from B to A with REL=relation. REV=made is sometimes used to identify the document author, either the author's e-mail address with a mailto URL, or a link to the author's home page.

Title

An advisory title for the linked resource. Here are some proposed relationship values:

`rel=top`

The link references the top of a hierarchy, *e.g.* the first or cover page in a collection.

`rel=contents`

The link references a document serving as a table of contents.

rel=index

The link references a document providing an index for the current document.

rel=glossary

The link references a document providing a glossary of terms that are relevant to the current document.

rel=copyright

The link references a copyright statement for the current document.

rel=next

The link references the next document to visit in a guided tour. It can be used, for example, to preload the next page.

rel=previous

The link references the previous document in a guided tour.

rel=help

The link references a document offering help, *e.g.* describing the wider context and offering further links to relevant documents. This is aimed at reorienting users who have lost their way.

rel=search

The link references a page for searching material related to a collection of pages

Example Link elements:

```
<LINK REL=Contents HREF=toc.html>
<LINK REL=Previous HREF=doc31.html>
<LINK REL=Next HREF=doc33.html>
<LINK REL=Chapter REV=Contents HREF=chapter.html>
```

THE BODY ELEMENT

This contains the document body. Both start and end tags for BODY may be omitted.

The body can contain a wide range of elements:

- Headings (H1–H6)
- The ADDRESS element
- Block level Elements
- Text level elements

The Key Attributes

Are: BACKGROUND, BGCOLOUR, TEXT, LINK, VLINK and ALINK. These can be used to set a repeating background image, plus background and foreground colours for normal text and hypertext links.

```
<!ENTITY% body.content"(%heading |%text |%block
   | ADDRESS)*">
<!ENTITY% colour"CDATA" -- a colour
   specification: #HHHHHH @@ details? -->
<!ENTITY% body-colour-attrs"
   bgcolour%colour #IMPLIED
  text%colour #IMPLIED
  link%colour #IMPLIED
  vlink%colour #IMPLIED
  alink%colour #IMPLIED
  ">
  <!ELEMENT BODY O O%body.content>
  <!ATTLIST BODY
  background%URL #IMPLIED -- texture tile for
  document background --
  %body-colour-attrs; -- bgcolour, text, link,
   vlink, alink --
  >
```

Example:

```
<body bgcolour=white text=black link=red
vlink=maroon alink=fuchsia>
```

Bgcolour

Specifies the background colour for the document body. See below for the syntax of colour values.

Text

Specifies the colour used to stroke the document's text. This is generally used when you have changed the background colour with the BGCOLOUR orBACKGROUND attributes.

Link

Specifies the colour used to stroke the text for unvisited hypertext links.

Vlink

Specifies the colour used to stroke the text for visited hypertext links.

Alink

Specifies the highlight colour used to stroke the text for hypertext links at the moment the user clicks on the link.

Background

Specifies a URL for an image that will be used to tile the document background.

Block and Text Level Elements

Most elements that can appear in the document body fall into one of two groups: block level elements which cause paragraph breaks, and text level elements which don't. Common block level elements include H1 to H6 (headers), P (paragraphs) LI (list items), and HR (horizontal rules). Common text level elements include EM, I, B and FONT (character emphasis), A (hypertext links), IMG and APPLET (embedded objects) and BR (line breaks).

Note that block elements generally act as containers for text level and other block level elements (excluding headings and address elements), while text level elements can only contain other text level elements. The exact model depends on the element.

Headings

```
<!--
There are six levels of headers from H1 (the
 most important)
to H6 (the least important).
-->

<!ELEMENT (%heading)-- (%text;)*>
<!ATTLIST (%heading)
          align (left|center|right) #IMPLIED
          >
```

H1, H2, H3, H4, H5 and H6 are used for document headings. You always need the start and end tags. H1 elements are more important than H2 elements and so on, so that H6 elements define the least important level of headings.

More important headings are generally rendered in a larger font than less important ones. Use the optional ALIGN attribute to set the text alignment within a heading, *e.g.*

```
<H1 ALIGN=CENTER>... centered heading... </H1>
```

The default is left alignment, but this can be overridden by an enclosing DIV or CENTER element.

ADDRESS

```
<!ENTITY% address.content"((%text;) | P)*">
<!ELEMENT ADDRESS--%address.content>
```

The ADDRESS element requires start and end tags, and specifies information such as authorship and contact details for the current document.

User agents should render the content with paragraph-breaks before and after. Note that the content is restricted to paragraphs, plain text and text-like elements as defined by the%text entity.

Example:

```
<ADDRESS>
Newsletter editor<BR>
J.R. Brown<BR>
8723 Buena Vista, Smallville, CT 01234<BR>
Tel: +1 (123) 456 7890
</ADDRESS>
```

Block Elements

- *Paragraphs*: The paragraph element requires a start tag, but the end tag can always be omitted. Use the ALIGN attribute to set the text alignment within a paragraph, *e.g.* <P ALIGN=RIGHT>
- *UL unordered lists*: These require start and end tags, and contain one or more LI elements representing individual list items.
- *OL ordered (i.e. numbered) lists*: These require start and

end tags, and contain one or more LI elements representing individual list items.

- *DL definition lists*: These require start and end tags and contain DT elements that give the terms, and DD elements that give corresponding definitions.
- *PRE preformatted text*: Requires start and end tags. These elements are rendered with a monospaced font and preserve layout defined by whitespace and line break characters.
- *DIV document divisions*: Requires start and end tags. It is used with the Aligm attribute to set the text alignment of the block elements it contains. Align can be one of left,center or right.
- *Center text alignment*: Requires start and end tags. It is used to center text lines enclosed by the center element. See DIV for a more general solution.
- Blockquote quoted passage: Requires start and end tags. It is used to enclose extended quotations and is typically rendered with indented margins.
- *Form fill-out forms*: Requires start and end tags. This element is used to define a fill-out form for processing by HTTP servers. The attributes are action, method and enctype. Form elements can't be nested.
- ISINDEX primitive HTML forms: Not a container, so the end tag is forbidden. This predates FORM and is used for simple kinds of forms which have a single text input field, implied by this element. A single ISINDEX can appear in the document head or body.
- *HR horizontal rules*: Not a container, so the end tag is forbidden. attributes are align, noshade, size and width.
- *Table can be nested*: Requires start and end tags. Each table starts with an optional caption followed by one or more TR elements defining table rows. Each row has one or more cells defined by TH or TD elements. attributes for table elements are width, border, cellspacing and cellpadding.

Paragraphs

```
<!ELEMENT P-O (%text)*>
<!ATTLIST P
align (left|center|right) #IMPLIED
>
```

The P element is used to markup paragraphs. It is a container and requires a start tag. The end tag is optional as it can always be inferred by the parser. User agents should place paragraph breaks before and after P elements. The rendering is user agent dependent, but text is generally wrapped to fit the space available.

Example:

```
<P>This is the first paragraph.
<P>This is the second paragraph.
```

Paragraphs are usually rendered flush left with a ragged right margin. The ALIGN attribute can be used to explicitly specify the horizontal alignment:

align=left

The paragraph is rendered flush left.

align=center

The paragraph is centered.

align=right

The paragraph is rendered flush right.

For example:

```
<p align=center>This is a centered paragraph.
<p align=right>and this is a flush right paragraph.
```

The default is left alignment, but this can be overridden by an enclosing DIV or CENTER element.

Lists

List items can contain block and text level items, including nested lists, although headings and address elements are excluded. This limitation is defined via the%flow entity.

Unordered Lists

```
<!ELEMENT UL-- (LI)+>
```

```
<!ENTITY% ULStyle"disc|square|circle">
<!ATTLIST UL -- unordered lists --
 type (%ULStyle) #IMPLIED -- bullet style --
 compact (compact) #IMPLIED -- reduced interitem
spacing --
 >
<!ELEMENT LI-O%flow -- list item -->
<!ATTLIST LI
 type (%LIStyle) #IMPLIED -- list item style -
-
 >
```

Unordered lists take the form:

```
<UL>
 <LI>... first list item
 <LI>... second list item
 ...
</UL>
```

The UL element is used for unordered lists. Both start and end tags are always needed. The LI element is used for individual list items. The end tag for LIelements can always be omitted. Note that LI elements can contain nested lists. The compact attribute can be used as a hint to the user agent to render lists in a more compact style.

The TYPE attribute can be used to set the bullet style on UL and LI elements. The permitted values are"disc","square" or"circle".

The default generally depends on the level of nesting for lists:

- With <li type=disc>
- With <li type=square>
  - With <li type=circle>

This list was chosen to cater for the original bullet shapes used by Mosaic in 1993.

Ordered (*i.e.* numbered) Lists

```
<!ELEMENT OL-- (LI)+>
<!ATTLIST OL -- ordered lists --
  type CDATA #IMPLIED -- numbering style --
  start NUMBER #IMPLIED -- starting sequence
```

```
number --
   compact (compact) #IMPLIED -- reduced interitem
spacing --
   >
<!ELEMENT LI-O%flow -- list item -->
<!ATTLIST LI
type CDATA #IMPLIED -- list item style --
value NUMBER #IMPLIED -- set sequence number --
>
```

Ordered (i.e. Numbered) Lists Take the form:

```
<OL>
  <LI>... first list item
  <LI>... second list item
  ...
</OL>
```

The OL START attribute can be used to initialize the sequence number (by default it is initialized to 1). You can set it later on with the VALUE attribute on LIelements. Both of these attributes expect integer values.

You can't indicate that numbering should be continued from a previous list, or to skip missing values without giving an explicit number.

Definition Lists

```
<!-- definition lists-DT for term, DD for its
definition -->
<!ELEMENT DL-- (DT|DD)+>
<!ATTLIST DL
   compact (compact) #IMPLIED -- more compact
style --
   >
<!ELEMENT DT-O (%text)*>
<!ELEMENT DD-O%flow;>
```

Definition lists take the form:

```
<DL>
  <DT> term name
  <DD> term definition
  ...
</DL>
```

DT elements can only act as containers for text level elements, while DD elements can hold block level elements as well, excluding headings and address elements.

For example:

```
<DL>
<DT>Term 1<dd>This is the definition of the first term.
<DT>Term 2<dd>This is the definition of the second term.
</DL>
```

which could be rendered as:

Term 1: This is the definition of the first term.

Term 2: This is the definition of the second term.

The COMPACT attribute can be used with the DL element as a hint to the user agent to render lists in a more compact style.

DIR and MENU

```
<!ELEMENT (DIR|MENU)-- (LI)+ -(%block)>
<!ATTLIST (DIR|MENU)
compact (compact) #IMPLIED
>
```

These elements have been part of HTML from the early days. They are intended for unordered lists similar to UL elements. User agents are recommended to render DIR elements as multicolumn directory lists, and MENU elements as single column menu lists. In practice, Mosaic and most other user agents have ignored this advice and instead render DIR and MENU in an identical way to UL elements.

Preformatted Text

```
<!ELEMENT PRE-- (%text)* -(%pre.exclusion)>
<!ATTLIST PRE
width NUMBER #implied
>
```

The PRE element can be used to include preformatted text. User agents render this in a fixed pitch font, preserving spacing associated with white space characters such as space and newline characters. Automatic word-wrap should be disabled within PRE elements. Note that the SGML standard requires that the parser remove a newline immediately following the start tag or immediately preceding the end tag.

PRE has the same content model as paragraphs, excluding images and elements that produce changes in font size, *e.g.* IMG, BIG, SMALL, SUB, SUP and FONT.

A few user agents support the WIDTH attribute. It provides a hint to the user agent of the required width in characters. The user agent can use this to select an appropriate *font size or to indent the content appropriately.*

Here is an example of a PRE element; a verse from Shelley (To a Skylark):

```
<PRE>
   Higher still and higher
    From the earth thou springest
   Like a cloud of fire;
    The blue deep thou wingest,
And singing still dost soar, and soaring ever
singest.
</PRE>
```

which is rendered as:

```
Higher still and higher
  From the earth thou springest
Like a cloud of fire;
  The blue deep thou wingest,
And singing still dost soar, and soaring ever
singest.
```

The horizontal tab character (encoded in Unicode, US ASCII and ISO 8859-1 as decimal 9) should be interpreted as the smallest non-zero number of spaces which will leave the number of characters so far on the line as a multiple of 8. Its use is strongly discouraged since it is common practice when editing to set the tab-spacing to other values, leading to misaligned documents.

XMP, LISTING and PLAINTEXT

```
<![%HTML.Deprecated [
<!ENTITY% literal"CDATA"
```

```
  -- historical, non-conforming parsing mode
 where
  the only markup signal is the end tag
  in full
  -->
<!ELEMENT (XMP|LISTING)--%literal>
<!ELEMENT PLAINTEXT-O%literal>
]]>
```

These are obsolete tags for preformatted text that predate the introduction of PRE. User agents may support these for backwards compatibility. Authors should avoid using them in new documents!

DIV and CENTER

```
<!ELEMENT DIV--%body.content>
<!ATTLIST DIV
    align  (left|center|right)  #IMPLIED  --
alignment of following text --
  >
<!-- CENTER is a shorthand for DIV with
ALIGN=CENTER -->
<!ELEMENT center--%body.content>
```

DIV elements can be used to structure HTML documents as a hierarchy of divisions. The ALIGN attribute can be used to set the default horizontal alignment for elements within the content of the DIV element. Its value is restricted to LEFT, CENTER or RIGHT, and is defined in the same way as for the paragraph element<P>.

Note that because DIV is a block-like element it will terminate an open P element. Other than this, user agents are not expected to render paragraph breaks before and after DIV elements. CENTER is directly equivalent to DIV with ALIGN=CENTER. Both DIV and CENTER require start and end tags. CENTER was introduced by Netscape before they added support for the HTML 3.0 DIV element. It is retained in HTML 3.2 on account of its widespread deployment.

BLOCKQUOTE

```
<!ELEMENT BLOCKQUOTE--%body.content>
```

HR–horizontal Rules

Horizontal rules may be used to indicate a change in topic. In a speech based user agent, the rule could be rendered as a pause.

```
<!ELEMENT HR-O EMPTY>
<!ATTLIST HR
   align (left|right|center) #IMPLIED
   noshade (noshade) #IMPLIED
   size%Pixels #IMPLIED
   width%Length #IMPLIED
   >
```

HR elements are not containers so the end tag is forbidden. The attributes are: ALIGN, NOSHADE, SIZE and WIDTH.

Align

This determines whether the rule is placed at the left, center or right of the space between the current left and right margins for align=left,align=center or align=right respectively. By default, the rule is centered.

Noshade

This attribute requests the user agent to render the rule in a solid colour rather than as the traditional two colour"groove".

Size

This can be used to set the height of the rule in pixels.

Width

This can be used to set the width of the rule in pixels (*e.g.* width=100) or as the percentage between the current left and right margins (*e.g.*width="50%"). The default is 100%.

Text Level Elements

These don't cause paragraph breaks. Text level elements that define character styles can generally be nested.

They can contain other text level elements but not block level elements:

- Font style elements

- Phrase elements
- Form Fields
- The A (anchor) element
- IMG–inline images
- APPLET (Java Applets)
- FONT elements
- BASEFONT elements
- BR–line breaks
- MAP–client-side image maps

Font Style Elements

These all require start and end tags, *e.g.*

```
This has some <B>bold text</B>.
```

Text level elements must be properly nested–the following is in error:

```
This has some <B>bold and <I></B>italic text
</I>.
```

User agents should do their best to respect nested emphasis, *e.g.*

```
This has some <B>bold and <I>italic text</I>
</B>.
```

Where the available fonts are restricted or for speech output, alternative means should be used for rendering differences in emphasis.

- TT teletype or monospaced text
- I italic text style
- B bold text style
- U underlined text style
- Strike strike-through text style
- Big places text in a large font
- Small places text in a small font
- Sub places text in subscript style
- Sup places text in superscript style

Note: future revisions to HTML may be phase out Strike in favour of the more concise"S" tag from HTML 3.0.

Phrase Elements

These all require start and end tags, *e.g.*

```
This has some <EM>emphasized text</EM>.
```

- EM basic emphasis typically rendered in an italic font
- Strong strong emphasis typically rendered in a bold font
- DFN defining instance of the enclosed term
- CODE used for extracts from programme code
- SAMP used for sample output from programmes, and scripts etc.
- KBD used for text to be typed by the user
- VAR used for variables or arguments to commands
- CITE used for citations or references to other sources

Form Fields

INPUT, SELECT and TEXTAREA are only allowed within FORM elements. INPUT can be used for a variety of form fields including single line text fields, password fields, checkboxes, radio buttons, submit and reset buttons, hidden fields, file upload, and image buttons. SELECT elements are used for single or multiple choice menus. TEXTAREA elements are used to define multi-line text fields. The content of the element is used to initialize the field.

DIFFERENT BROWSERS

According to browser statistics the current usage pattern includes:

- 124 versions of Microsoft Internet Explorer (88.0% market share)
- 42 versions of Netscape Navigator (9.2% market share)
- 23 versions of Opera (1.2% market share)
- 204 others (1.6% market share)

The many versions arise from:

- Different releases
- Different platforms

Well-written Web pages work well on all reasonably new browsers.

- "This page is optimized for XYZ" ="I only tested this page on XYZ"

- "This page is best viewed in 1024x768" ="my screen has resolution 1024x768"
- Of course, advanced functionality (JavaScript, XSLT...) may require the newest browser releases

BROWSERS ARE FORGIVING

Most HTML documents are in fact not valid:

- Authors are careless
- Documents are"validated" by viewing them in a browser
- Autogenerated HTML is often invalid

STRUCTURING GENERAL INFORMATION

There are many problems with this approach to using HTML:

- The semantics is encoded into text formatting tags
- There is no means of checking that a recipe is encoded correctly
- It is difficult to change the layout of recipes (CSS is not enough)

PROBLEMS WITH HTML

- *The language is by design hardwired to describe hypertext*:
  - There is a fixed collection of tags with a fixed semantics
  - But much information just is not hypertext!
- *Syntax and semantics is mixed together*:
  - The structuring of data dictates its presentation in browsers
  - Stylesheets only provide a weak solution
  - Different views are not supported
- The standards have been undermined:
  - Most HTML documents are invalid
  - The browsers define sloppy ad-hoc standards

4

Namespaces, XInclude and XML Base

NAMESPACES–MIXING XML LANGUAGES

MIXING XML LANGUAGES

Consider an XML language WidgetML which uses XHTML as a sublanguage for help messages:

```
<widget type="gadget">
  <head size="medium"/>
  <big><subwidget ref="gizmo"/></big>
  <info>
   <head>
    <title>Description of gadget</title>
   </head>
  <body>
    <h1>Gadget</h1>
    A gadget contains a big gizmo
   </body>
  </info>
</widget>
```

A problem: the meaning of head and big depends on the context! This complicates things for processors and might even cause ambiguities. The root of the problem is: one common name space.

QUALIFYING NAMES

Simple solution: qualify names with URIs (Universal Resource Identifiers)

```
<{http://www.w3.org/TR/xhtml1}head>
\                           /\ /
------------------------- --
  qualifying URI        local name
```

Do not be confused by the use of URIs for namespaces:

- They are not supposed to point to anything
- It is simply the cheapest way of getting unique names
- We rely on existing organizations that control domain names

NAMESPACE DECLARATIONS

Namespaces are declared by special attributes and associated prefixes:

```
<... xmlns:foo="http://www.w3.org/TR/xhtml1">
  ...
  <foo:head>...</foo:head>
  ...
</...>
```

xmlns:prefix="URI" declares a namespace with a prefix and a URI:

- The scope of declaration is lexical, the element containing the declaration and all descendants can be overridden by nested declaration
- Both element and attribute names can be qualified with namespaces
- The name of the prefix is irrelevant–applications should use only the URI

For backward compatibility and simplicity, unprefixed element names are assigned a default namespace:

- *Declaration*: xmlns="URI"
- *Default value*:"" (means: treat as unqualified name)
- Does not affect unprefixed attribute names (they belong to the containing elements)

WidgetML with namespaces:

```
<widget xmlns="http://www.widget.org"
        xmlns:xhtml="http://www.w3.org/TR/xhtml1"
        type="gadget">
   <head size="medium"/>
```

```
  <big><subwidget ref="gizmo"/></big>
  <info>
   <xhtml:head>
    <xhtml:title>Description of gadget</
   xhtml:title>
  </xhtml:head>
  <xhtml:body>
    <xhtml:h1>Gadget</xhtml:h1>
    A gadget contains a big gizmo
  </xhtml:body>
 </info>
</widget>
```

NAMESPACES IN XML

We envision applications of Extensible Markup Language (XML) where a single XML document may contain elements and attributes (here referred to as a"markup vocabulary") that are defined for and used by multiple software modules. One motivation for this is modularity: if such a markup vocabulary exists which is well-understood and for which there is useful software available, it is better to re-use this markup rather than re-invent it.

Such documents, containing multiple markup vocabularies, pose problems of recognition and collision. Software modules need to be able to recognize the elements and attributes which they are designed to process, even in the face of"collisions" occurring when markup intended for some other software package uses the same element name or attribute name.

These considerations require that document constructs should have names constructed so as to avoid clashes between names from different markup vocabularies. This specification describes a mechanism, XML namespaces, which accomplishes this by assigning expanded names to elements and attributes.

A Note on Notation and Usage

Where emphasized, the key words must, must not, required, should, should not, may in this document are to be interpreted as described in [Keywords]. Note that many of the nonterminals in the productions in this specification are defined not here but in the XML specification [XML]. When nonterminals defined here have the same names as nonterminals defined in the XML specification, the productions here in all cases match a subset of the strings matched by the corresponding ones there.

In this document's productions, the NSC is a"Namespace Constraint", one of the rules that documents conforming to this specification must follow.

XML NAMESPACES

Basic Concepts

Definition An XML namespace is identified by a URI reference [RFC3986]; element and attribute names may be placed in an XML namespace using the mechanisms described in this specification.

[Definition: An expanded name is a pair consisting of a namespace name and a local name.] [Definition: For a name N in a namespace identified by a URI I, the namespace name is I. For a name N that is not in a namespace, the namespace namehas no value.] [Definition: In either case the local name is N.] It is this combination of the universally managed IRI namespace with the vocabulary's local names that is effective in avoiding name clashes.

URI references can contain characters not allowed in names, and are often inconveniently long, so expanded names are not used directly to name elements and attributes in XML documents. Instead qualified names are used. [Definition: A qualified name is a name subject to namespace interpretation.] In documents conforming to this specification, element and attribute names appear as qualified names.

Syntactically, they are either prefixed names or unprefixed names. An attribute-based declaration syntax is provided to bind prefixes to namespace names and to bind a default namespace that applies to unprefixed element names; these declarations are scoped by the elements on which they appear so that different bindings may apply in different parts of a document. Processors conforming to this specification must recognize and act on these declarations and prefixes.

Use of URIs as Namespace Names

The empty string, though it is a legal URI reference, cannot be used as a namespace name. The use of relative URI references, including same-document references, in namespace declarations is deprecated.

Note: This deprecation of relative URI references was decided on by a W3C XML Plenary Ballot [Relative URI deprecation]. It also declares that"later specifications such as DOM, XPath, etc. will define no interpretation for them".

Comparing URI References

URI references identifying namespaces are compared when determining whether a name belongs to a given namespace, and whether two names belong to the same namespace. [Definition: The two URIs are treated as strings, and they are identical if and only if the strings are identical, that is, if they are the same sequence of characters.] The comparison is case-sensitive, and no%-escaping is done or undone.

A consequence of this is that URI references which are not identical in this sense may resolve to the same resource. Examples include URI references which differ only in case or%-escaping, or which are in external entities which have different base URIs (but note that relative URIs are deprecated as namespace names).

In a namespace declaration, the URI reference is the normalized value of the attribute, so replacement of XML character and entity references has already been done before any comparison.

Examples:

The URI references below are all different for the purposes of identifying namespaces, since they differ in case:

```
" http://www.example.org/wine
" http://www.Example.org/wine
```

" **http://www.example.org/Wine**

The IRI references below are also all different for the purposes of identifying namespaces:

" **http://www.example.org/~wilbur**

" **http://www.example.org/%7ewilbur**

" **http://www.example.org/%7Ewilbur**

Because of the risk of confusion between URIs that would be equivalent if dereferenced, the use of%-escaped characters in namespace names is strongly discouraged.

DECLARING NAMESPACES

Definition: A namespace (or more precisely, a namespace binding) is declared using a family of reserved attributes. Such an attribute's name must either be xmlns or begin xmlns:. These attributes, like any other XML attributes, may be provided directly or by default.

The attribute's normalized value must be either a URI reference–the namespace name identifying the namespace–or an empty string.

The namespace name, to serve its intended purpose, should have the characteristics of uniqueness and persistence. It is not a goal that it be directly usable for retrieval of a schema (if any exists). Uniform Resource Names [RFC2141]is an example of a syntax that is designed with these goals in mind. However, it should be noted that ordinary URLs can be managed in such a way as to achieve these same goals.

[*Definition*: If the attribute name matches Prefixed AttName, then the NCName gives the namespace prefix, used to associate element and attribute names with the namespace name in the attribute value in the scope of the element to which the declaration is attached. In such declarations, the namespace name may not be empty.]

[*Definition*: If the attribute name matches DefaultAttName, then the namespace name in the attribute value is that of the default namespace in the scope of the element to which the declaration is attached.] Default namespaces and overriding of declarations are discussed in 6 Applying Namespaces to Elements and Attributes.

An example namespace declaration, which associates the namespace prefix edi with the namespace namehttp://ecommerce.example.org/schema:

```
<x xmlns:edi='http://ecommerce.example.org/schema'>
 <!-- the"edi" prefix is bound to http://ecommerce.example.org/schema
      for the"x" element and contents -->
</x>
```

Namespace Constraint

Reserved Prefixes and Namespace Names: The prefix xml is by definition bound to the namespace name http://www.w3.org/XML/1998/namespace. It may, but need not, be declared, and must not be bound to any other namespace name. Other prefixes must not be bound to this namespace name, and it must not be declared as the default namespace.

The prefix xmlns is used only to declare namespace bindings and is by definition bound to the namespace namehttp://www.w3.org/2000/xmlns/. It must not be declared. Other prefixes must not be bound to this namespace name, and it must not be declared as the default namespace. Element names must not have the prefix xmlns. All other prefixes beginning with the three-letter sequence x, m, l, in any case combination, are reserved.

This means that:

- Users should not use them except as defined by later specifications
- Processors must not treat them as fatal errors.

Though they are not themselves reserved, it is inadvisable to use prefixed names whose LocalPart begins with the letters x, m, l, in any case combination, as these names would be reserved if used without a prefix.

QUALIFIED NAMES

In XML documents conforming to this specification, some names (constructs corresponding to the nonterminal Name) must begiven as qualified names, defined as follows:

Qualified Name

```
QName                  ::=  PrefixedName
                            | UnprefixedName
PrefixedName   ::=  Prefix':' LocalPart
UnprefixedName::=  LocalPart
Prefix                 ::=  NCName
LocalPart              ::=  NCName
```

The Prefix provides the namespace prefix part of the qualified name, and must be associated with a namespace URI reference in a namespace declaration. [Definition: The LocalPart provides the local part of the qualified name.]

Note that the prefix functions only as a placeholder for a namespace name. Applications should use the namespace name, not the prefix, in constructing names whose scope extends beyond the containing document.

USING QUALIFIED NAMES

In XML documents conforming to this specification, element names are given as qualified names, as follows:

Element Names

STag	::=	'<' QName (S Attribute)* S? '>'	[NSC: Prefix Declared]
ETag	::=	'</' QName S? '>'	[NSC: Prefix Declared]
EmptyElemTag	::=	'<' QName (S Attribute)* S? '/>'	[NSC: Prefix Declared]

An example of a qualified name serving as an element name:

```
<!-- the'price' element's namespace is
http://ecommerce.example.org/schema -->
<edi:price xmlns:edi='http://ecommerce.
example.org/schema' units='Euro'>32.18</edi:price>
```

Attributes are either namespace declarations or their names are given as qualified names:

Attribute

```
Attribute  ::= NSAttName Eq AttValue
```

```
                | QName Eq AttValue [NSC: Prefix
                                     Declared]
```

An example of a qualified name serving as an attribute name:

```
<x xmlns:edi='http://ecommerce.example.org/
      schema'>
<!-- the'taxClass' attribute's namespace is
      http://ecommerce.example.org/schema -->
<lineItem edi:taxClass="exempt">Baby food</
      lineItem>
</x>
```

Namespace Constraint: Prefix Declared

The namespace prefix, unless it is xml or xmlns, must have been declared in a namespace declaration attribute in either the start-tag of the element where the prefix is used or in an ancestor element (*i.e.* an element in whose content the prefixed markup occurs).

This constraint may lead to operational difficulties in the case where the namespace declaration attribute is provided, not directly in the XML document entity, but via a default attribute declared in an external entity. Such declarations may not be read by software which is based on a non-validating XML processor. Many XML applications, presumably including namespace-sensitive ones, fail to require validating processors. If correct operation with such applications is required, namespace declarations mustbe provided either directly or via default attributes declared in the internal subset of the DTD.

Element names and attribute names are also given as qualified names when they appear in declarations in the DTD.

APPLYING NAMESPACES TO ELEMENTS AND ATTRIBUTES

Namespace Scoping

The scope of a namespace declaration declaring a prefix extends from the beginning of the start-tag in which it appears to the end of the corresponding end-tag, excluding the scope of any inner declarations with the same NSAttName part. In the case of an empty tag, the scope is the tag itself.

Such a namespace declaration applies to all element and attribute names within its scope whose prefix matches that specified in the declaration.

The expanded name corresponding to a prefixed element or attribute name has the URI to which the prefix is bound as its namespace name, and the local part as its local name.

```
<?xml version="1.0"?>
<html:html xmlns:html='http://www.w3.org/1999/
xhtml'>
  <html:head><html:title>Frobnostication</
    html:title></html:head>
  <html:body><html:p>Moved to
  <html:a href='http://frob.example.com'>here.</
    html:a></html:p></html:body>
</html:html>
```

Multiple namespace prefixes can be declared as attributes of a single element, as shown in this example:

```
<?xml version="1.0"?>
<!-- both namespace prefixes are available
   throughout -->
<bk:book xmlns:bk='urn:loc.gov:books'
     xmlns:isbn='urn:ISBN:0-395-36341-6'>
   <bk:title>Cheaper by the Dozen</bk:title>
   <isbn:number>1568491379</isbn:number>
</bk:book>
```

NAMESPACE DEFAULTING

The scope of a default namespace declaration extends from the beginning of the start-tag in which it appears to the end of the corresponding end-tag, excluding the scope of any inner default namespace declarations. In the case of an empty tag, the scope is the tag itself.

A default namespace declaration applies to all unprefixed element names within its scope. Default namespace declarations do not apply directly to attribute names; the interpretation of unprefixed attributes is determined by the element on which they appear. If there is a default namespace declaration in scope, the expanded name corresponding to an unprefixed element name has the URI of the default namespace as its namespace name.

If there is no default namespace declaration in scope, the namespace name has no value. The namespace name for an unprefixed attribute name always has no value. In all cases, the local name islocal part (which is of course the same as the unprefixed name itself).

```
<?xml version="1.0"?>
<!-- elements are in the HTML namespace, in
   this case by default -->
<html xmlns='http://www.w3.org/1999/xhtml'>
   <head><title>Frobnostication</title></head>
   <body><p>Moved to
      <a href='http://frob.example.com'>here</
     a>.</p></body>
</html>

<?xml version="1.0"?>
<!-- unprefixed element types are from"books" -
    ->
<book xmlns='urn:loc.gov:books'
    xmlns:isbn='urn:ISBN:0-395-36341-6'>
      <title>Cheaper by the Dozen</title>
      <isbn:number>1568491379</isbn:number>
</book>
```

A larger example of namespace scoping:

```
<?xml version="1.0"?>
<!-- initially, the default namespace is"books"
   -->
   <book xmlns='urn:loc.gov:books'
      xmlns:isbn='urn:ISBN:0-395-36341-6'>
   <title>Cheaper by the Dozen</title>
   <isbn:number>1568491379</isbn:number>
   <notes>
      <!-- make HTML the default namespace for
      some commentary -->
```

```
      <p xmlns='http://www.w3.org/1999/xhtml'>
        This is a <i>funny</i> book!
      </p>
  </notes>
</book>
```

The attribute value in a default namespace declaration may be empty. This has the same effect, within the scope of the declaration, of there being no default namespace.

```
<?xml version='1.0'?>
<Beers>
  <!-- the default namespace inside tables is
      that of HTML -->
  <table xmlns='http://www.w3.org/1999/xhtml'>
  <th><td>Name</td><td>Origin</
    td><td>Description</td></th>
  <tr>
    <!-- no default namespace inside table cells
    -->
    <td><brandName xmlns="">Huntsman</
       brandName></   td>
    <td><origin xmlns="">Bath, UK</origin></td>
    <td>
      <details xmlns=""><class>Bitter</
         class><hop>Fuggles</hop>
        <pro>Wonderful hop, light alcohol, good
            summer beer</pro>
        <con>Fragile; excessive variance pub
            to pub</con>
        </details>
      </td>
   </tr>
 </table>
</Beers>
```

Uniqueness of Attributes

In XML documents conforming to this specification, no tag may contain two attributes which:

1. Have identical names, or

2. Have qualified names with the same local part and with prefixes which have been bound to namespace names that are identical.

This constraint is equivalent to requiring that no element have two attributes with the same expanded name.

For example, each of the bad empty-element tags is illegal in the following:

```
<!-- http://www.w3.org is bound to n1 and n2 -->
<x xmlns:n1="http://www.w3.org"
   xmlns:n2="http://www.w3.org" >
  <bad a="1" a="2"/>
  <bad n1:a="1" n2:a="2"/>
</x>
```

However, each of the following is legal, the second because the default namespace does not apply to attribute names:

```
<!-- http://www.w3.org is bound to n1 and is
    the default -->
<x xmlns:n1="http://www.w3.org"
   xmlns="http://www.w3.org" >
   <good a="1" b="2"/>
   <good a="1" n1:a="2"/>
</x>
```

CONFORMANCE OF DOCUMENTS

This specification applies to XML 1.0 documents. To conform to this specification, a document must be well-formed according to the XML 1.0 specification [XML10].

In XML documents which conform to this specification, element and attribute names must match the production for QName andmust satisfy the"Namespace Constraints". All other tokens in the document which are required, for XML 1.0 well-formedness, to match the XML production for Name must match this specification's production for NCName.

[*Definition:* A document is namespace-well-formed if it conforms to this specification.]

It follows that in a namespace-well-formed document:

- All element and attribute names contain either zero or one colon;

- No entity names, processing instruction targets, or notation names contain any colons.

In addition, a namespace-well-formed document may also be namespace-valid.

[*Definition*: A namespace-well-formed document is namespace-valid if it is valid according to the XML 1.0 specification, and all tokens other than element and attribute names which are required, for XML 1.0 validity, to match the XML production for Name match this specification's production for NCName.]

It follows that in a namespace-valid document:

- No attributes with a declared type of ID, IDREF(S), ENTITY(IES), or NOTATION contain any colons.

CONFORMANCE OF PROCESSORS

To conform to this specification, a processor must report violations of namespace well-formedness, with the exception that it is not required to check that namespace names are legal URIs.

[*Definition*: A validating XML processor that conforms to this specification is namespace-validating if in addition it reports violations of namespace validity.]

A Normative References

Keywords

RFC 2119: Key words for use in RFCs to Indicate Requirement Levels, S. Bradner, ed. IETF (Internet Engineering Task Force), March 1997. Available at http://www.rfc-editor.org/rfc/rfc2119.txt

RFC2141

RFC 2141: URN Syntax, R. Moats, ed. IETF (Internet Engineering Task Force), May 1997. Available at http://www.rfc-editor.org/rfc/rfc2141.txt.

RFC3986

RFC 3986: Uniform Resource Identifier (URI): Generic

Syntax, T. Berners-Lee, R. Fielding, and L. Masinter, eds. IETF (Internet Engineering Task Force), January 2005. Available at http://www.rfc-editor.org/rfc/rfc3986.txt

RFC3629

RFC 3629: UTF-8, a transformation format of ISO 10646, F. Yergeau, ed. IETF (Internet Engineering Task Force), November 2003. Available at http://www.rfc-editor.org/rfc/rfc3629.txt

XML

Extensible Markup Language (XML) 1.0 (Fourth Edition), Tim Bray, Jean Paoli, C. M. Sperberg-McQueen, Eve Maler, and François Yergeau eds. W3C (World Wide Web Consortium), 16 August 2006. Available at http://www.w3.org/TR/2006/REC-xml-20060816/.

B Other references (Non-Normative)

1.0 Errata

Namespaces in XML Errata. W3C (World Wide Web Consortium). Available at http://www.w3.org/XML/xml-names-19990114-errata.

Relative URI deprecation

Results of W3C XML Plenary Ballot on relative URI References In namespace declarations 3-17 July 2000, Dave Hollander and C. M. Sperberg-McQueen, 6 September 2000. Available at http://www.w3.org/2000/09/xppa.

C The Internal Structure of XML Namespaces (Non-Normative)

This appendix has been deleted.

D Changes since version 1.0 (Non-Normative)

This version incorporates the errata as of 1 June 2006 [1.0 Errata]. There are several editorial changes, including a number of terminology changes and additions intended to produce greater consistency. The non-normative appendix"The Internal Structure of XML Namespaces" has been removed.

E Acknowledgements (Non-Normative)

This work reflects input from a very large number of people, including especially the participants in the World Wide Web Consortium XML Working Group and Special Interest Group and the participants in the W3C Metadata Activity. The contributions of Charles Frankston of Microsoft were particularly valuable.

SPECIFICATION CONTROVERSIES

How should a relative URI be interpreted?:

- Relative to the base URI?
- Relative to the document URI?
- Just as a string?

This innocent question spawned a controversy that resulted in leaving the matter undefined (by deprecating such namespaces).

Other controversies:

- Does the choice of prefix matter, or is

```
<a:widget xmlns:a="www.widget.org"/> the same as
<b:widget xmlns:b="www.widget.org"/>?
```

- Is <a:widget size="big"/> the same as

```
<a:widget a:size="big"/>?
```

Unfortunately, according to the spec, the choice of prefix may matter, and an unqualified attribute generally does not just inherit the namespace from its element.

XINCLUDE–COMBINING XML DOCUMENTS

INTRODUCTION

Many programming languages provide an inclusion mechanism to facilitate modularity. Markup languages also often have need of such a mechanism.

This specification introduces a generic mechanism for merging XML documents (as represented by their information sets) for use by applications that need such a facility. The syntax leverages existing XML constructs–elements, attributes, and URI references.

Relationship to XLink

XInclude differs from the linking features described in the [XML Linking Language], specifically links with the attribute valueshow="embed". Such links provide a media-type independent syntax for indicating that a resource is to be embedded graphically within the display of the document. XLink does not specify a specific processing model, but simply facilitates the detection of links and recognition of associated metadata by a higher level application.

XInclude, on the other hand, specifies a media-type specific (XML into XML) transformation. It defines a specific processing model for merging information sets. XInclude processing occurs at a low level, often by a generic XInclude processor which makes the resulting information set available to higher level applications.

Simple information item inclusion as described in this specification differs from transclusion, which preserves contextual information such as style.

Relationship to XML External Entities

There are a number of differences between XInclude and [XML 1.0] or [XML 1.1] external entities which make them complementary technologies.

Processing of external entities (as with the rest of DTDs) occurs at parse time. XInclude operates on information sets and thus is orthogonal to parsing.

Declaration of external entities requires a DTD or internal subset. This places a set of dependencies on inclusion, for instance, the syntax for the DOCTYPE declaration requires that the document element be named–orthogonal to inclusion in many cases. Validating parsers must have a complete content model defined. XInclude is orthogonal to validation and the name of the document element.

External entities provide a level of indirection–the external entity must be declared and named, and separately invoked.

XInclude uses direct references. Applications which generate XML output incrementally can benefit from not having to pre-declare inclusions.

Failure to load an external entity is normally a fatal error. XInclude allows the author to provide default content that will be used if the remote resource cannot be loaded.

The syntax for an internal subset is cumbersome to many authors of simple well-formed XML documents. XInclude syntax is based on familiar XML constructs.

Relationship to DTDs

XInclude defines no relationship to DTD validation. XInclude describes an infoset-to-infoset transformation and not a change in XML parsing behaviour. XInclude does not define a mechanism for DTD validation of the resulting infoset.

Relationship to XML Schemas

XInclude defines no relationship to the augmented infosets produced by applying an XML schema. Such an augmented infoset can be supplied as the input infoset, or such augmentation might be applied to the infoset resulting from the inclusion.

Relationship to Grammar-Specific Inclusions

Special-purpose inclusion mechanisms have been introduced into specific XML grammars. XInclude provides a generic mechanism for recognizing and processing inclusions, and as such can offer a simpler overall authoring experience, greater performance, and less code redundancy.

TERMINOLOGY

Definition: The key words must, must not, required, shall, shall not, should, should not, recommended, may, andoptional in this specification are to be interpreted as described in [IETF RFC 2119].

Definition: The term information set refers to the output of an [XML 1.0] or [XML 1.1] processor, expressed as a collection of information items and properties as defined by the [XML Information Set] specification.] In this document the term infoset is used as a synonym for information set.

Definition: The term fatal error refers to the presence of factors that prevent normal processing from continuing.] [Definition: The term resource error refers to a failure of an attempt to fetch a resource from a URL. XInclude processors must stop processing when encountering errors other than resource errors, which must be handled as described in 4.4 Fallback Behaviour.

SYNTAX

XInclude defines a namespace associated with the URI. The XInclude namespace contains two elements with the local names include and fallback. For convenience, within this specification these elements are referred to as xi:include and xi:fallback respectively.

XI:include Element

The xi:include element has the following attributes:

Hhref

A value which, after appropriate escaping (4.1.1 Escaping of href attribute values) has been performed, results in a URI reference or an IRI reference specifying the location of the resource to include. The href attribute is optional; the absence of this attribute is the same as specifying href="", that is, the reference is to the same document. If the hrefattribute is absent when parse="xml", the xpointer attribute must be present. Fragment identifiers must not be used; their appearance is a fatal error. A value that results in a syntactically invalid URI or IRI should be reported as a fatal error, but some implementations may find it impractical to distinguish this case from a resource error.

Note: A URI ending in # is considered by [IETF RFC 2396] to have an empty fragment identifier. Such a URI would result in afatal error as described above.

Note: A key feature of XInclude is that it allows a resource to be cast to a user-specifed type for inclusion (XML or text).

The returned media type is therefore essentially ignored for the purposes of inclusion processing, and the syntax of the fragment identifier of the returned media type will generally not be applicable to the user-specified type.

Forparse="xml" inclusions, sub-resources are identified by a separate xpointer attribute, which is applied after the casting takes place.

While this does not prevent subresources of XML documents to be identified by URI (Architecture of the World Wide Web [Identification]), it does preclude the use of these identifiers directly within XInclude.

Parse

Indicates whether to include the resource as parsed XML or as text. The parse attribute allows XInclude to give the author of the including document priority over the server of the included document in terms of how to process the included content. A value of"xml" indicates that the resource must be parsed as XML and the infosets merged.

A value of"text" indicates that the resource must be included as the character information items. This attribute is optional. When omitted, the value of"xml" is implied (even in the absence of a default value declaration). Values other than"xml" and"text" are a fatal error.

Note: For interoperability between validating and non-validating systems, whitespace should not appear in the parse attribute.

Xpointer

When parse="xml", the XPointer ([XPointer Framework]) contained in the xpointer attribute is evaluated to identify a portion of the resource to include. This attribute is optional; when omitted, the entire resource is included. The xpointerattribute must not be present when parse="text". If the xpointer attribute is absent, the href attribute must be present.

Note: Since the xpointer attribute is not a URI reference, and%-escaping is not done in XPointers,'%' is an ordinary character in the value of the xpointer attribute.

Encoding

When parse="text", it is sometimes impossible to correctly detect the encoding of the text resource. The encoding attribute specifies how the resource is to be translated. The value of this attribute should be a valid encoding name. The encodingattribute has no effect when parse="xml".

Accept

The value of the accept attribute may be used by the XInclude processor to aid in content negotiation. When the XInclude processor fetches a resource via HTTP, it should place the value of the accept attribute, if one exists, in the HTTP request as an Accept header as described in section 14.1 of [IETF RFC 2616]. Values containing characters outside the range #x20 through #x7E must be flagged as fatal errors.

Accept-language

The value of the accept-language attribute may be used by the XInclude processor to aid in content negotiation. When the XInclude processor fetches a resource via HTTP, it should place the value of the accept-language attribute, if one exists, in the HTTP request as an Accept-Language header as described in section 14.4 of [IETF RFC 2616]. Values containing characters outside the range #x20 through #x7E are disallowed in HTTP headers, and must be flagged as fatal errors.

Attributes other than those listed above may be placed on the xi:include element. Unprefixed attribute names are reserved for future versions of this specification, and must be ignored by XInclude 1.0 processors.

The children property of the xi:include element may include a single xi:fallback element; the appearance of more than onexi:fallback element, an xi:include element, or any other element from the XInclude namespace is a fatal error. Other content (text, processing instructions, comments, elements not in the XInclude namespace, descendants of child elements) is not constrained by this specification and is ignored by the XInclude processor, that is, it has no effect on include processing, and does not appear in the children properties of the result infoset. Such content might be used by applications analyzing a pre-inclusion infoset, or be made available to an application post-inclusion through means other than the normal infoset properties.

XI:fallback Element

The xi:fallback element appears as a child of an xi:include element. It provides a mechanism for recovering from missing resources. When a resource error is encountered, the xi:include element is replaced with the contents of the xi:fallbackelement. If the xi:fallback element is empty, the xi:include element is removed from the result. If the xi:fallback element is missing, a resource error results in a fatal error.

The xi:fallback element can appear only as a child of an xi:include element. It is a fatal error for an xi:fallback element to appear in a document anywhere other than as the direct child of the xi:include (before inclusion processing on the contents of the element.) It is a fatal error for the xi:fallback element to contain any elements from the XInclude namespace other thanxi:include.

Attributes may be placed on the xi:fallback element. Unprefixed attribute names are reserved for future versions of this specification, and must be ignored by XInclude 1.0 processors.

The content of xi:fallback elements are ignored unless a resource error occurs while processing the surrounding xi:includeelement. In particular, apparent fatal errors caused by the presence, absence, or content of elements and attributes inside thexi:fallback element must not be reported in xi:fallback elements that are ignored.

PROCESSING MODEL

Inclusion as defined in this document is a specific type of [XML Information Set] transformation.

[Definition: The input for the inclusion transformation consists of a source infoset.] [Definition: The output, called the result infoset, is a new infoset which merges the source infoset with the infosets of resources identified by URI references or

IRI references appearing in xi:include elements.] Thus a mechanism to resolve URIs or IRIs and return the identified resources as infosets is assumed. Well-formed XML entities that do not have defined infosets (*e.g.* an external entity with multiple top-level elements) are outside the scope of this specification, either for use as a source infoset or the result infoset.

xi:include elements in the source infoset serve as inclusion transformation instructions. [Definition: The information items located by the xi:include element are called the top-level included items]. [Definition: The top-level included items together with their attributes, namespaces, and descendants, are called the included items]. The result infoset is essentially a copy of the source infoset, with each xi:include element and its descendants replaced by its corresponding included items.

The Include Location

The value of the href attribute, after escaping according to 4.1.1 Escaping of href attribute values, is interpreted as either a URI reference or an IRI reference. The base URI for relative URIs or IRIs is the base URI of the xi:include element as specified in[XML Base].

[Definition: The URI or IRI resulting from resolution of the normalized value of the href attribute (or the empty string if no attribute appears) to absolute URI or IRI form is called the include location.]

The absence of a value for the href attribute, either by the appearance of href="" or by the absence of the href attribute, represents a case which may be incompatible with certain implementation strategies.

For instance, an XInclude processor might not have a textual representation of the source infoset to include as parse="text", or it may be unable to access another part of the document using parse="xml" and an xpointer because of streamability concerns. An implementation may choose to treat any or all absences of a value for the href attribute as resource errors. Implementations should document the conditions under which such resource errors occur.

Escaping of Href Attribute Values

The value of this attribute is an XML resource identifer as defined in [XML 1.1] section 4.2.2"External Entities", which is interpreted as [Definition: an IRI Reference as defined in RFC 3987 [IETF RFC 3987]], after the escaping procedure described in[XML 1.1] section 4.2.2 is applied. If necessary for the implementation, the value may be further converted to a URI reference as described in [XML 1.1].

Using XInclude with Content Negotiation

The use of a mechanism like HTTP [IETF RFC 2616] content negotiation introduces an additional level of potential complexity into the use of XInclude.

Developers who use XInclude in situations where content negotiation is likely or possible should be aware of the possibility that they will be including content that may differ structurally from the content they expected, even if that content is XML.

For example, a single URI or IRI may variously return a raw XML representation of the resource, an XSL-FO [XSL-FO]representation, or an XHTML [XHTML] representation, as well as versions in different character encodings or languages.

Authors whose XInclude processing depends on the receipt of a particular vocabulary of XML should use the accept and accept-language attributes to increase the probability that the resource is provided in the expected format.

Included Items when parse="xml"

When parse="xml", the include location is dereferenced, the resource is fetched, and an infoset is created by parsing the resource as if the media type were application/xml (including character encoding determination).

Note: The specifics of how an infoset is created are intentionally unspecified, to allow for flexibility by implementations and to avoid defining a particular processing model for components of the XML architecture. Particulars of whether DTD or XML schema validation are performed, for example, are not constrained by this specification.

Note: The character encodings of the including and included resources can be different. This does not affect the resulting infoset, but might need to be taken into account during any subsequent serialization.

Resources that are unavailable for any reason (for example the resource doesn't exist, connection difficulties or security restrictions prevent it from being fetched, the URI scheme isn't a fetchable one, the resource is in an unsupported encoding, or the resource is determined through implementation-specific mechanisms not to be XML) result in a resource error. Resources that contain non-well-formed XML result in a fatal error.

Note: The distinction between a resource error and a fatal error is somewhat implementation-dependent. Consider an include location returning an HTML document, perhaps as an error page. One processor might determine that no infoset can be created from the resource (by examining the media type, for example) and raise a resource error, enabling fallback behaviour. Another processor with no such heuristics might attempt to parse the non-XML resource as XML and encounter a well-formedness (fatal) error.

[Definition: xi:include elements in this infoset are recursively processed to create the acquired infoset. For an intra-document reference (via xpointer attribute) the source infoset is used as the acquired infoset.]

[Definition: The portion of the acquired infoset to be included is called the inclusion target.] The document information item of the acquired infoset serves as the inclusion target unless the xpointer attribute is present and identifies a subresource. XPointers of the forms described in [XPointer Framework] and [XPointer element() scheme] must be supported. XInclude processors optionally support other forms of XPointer such as that described in [XPointer xpointer() Scheme]. An error in the XPointer is aresource error.

The [XPointer xpointer() Scheme] is not specified in terms of the [XML Information Set], but instead is based on the [XPath 1.0]Data Model, because the XML Information Set had not yet been developed. The mapping between XPath node locations and information items is straightforward. However, xpointer() assumes that all entities have been expanded. Thus it is a fatal error to attempt to resolve an xpointer() scheme on a document that contains unexpanded entity reference information items. The set of top-level included items is derived from the acquired infoset as follows.

Document Information Items

The inclusion target might be a document information item (for instance, no specified xpointer attribute, or an XPointer specifically locating the document root.) In this case, the set of top-level included items is the children of the acquired infoset'sdocument information item, except for the document type declaration information item child, if one exists.

Note: The XML Information Set specification does not provide for preservation of white space outside the document element. XInclude makes no further provision to preserve this white space.

Multiple Nodes

The inclusion target might consist of more than a single node. In this case the set of top-level included items is the set of information items from the acquired infoset corresponding to the nodes referred to by the XPointer, in the order in which they appear in the acquired infoset.

Range Locations

The inclusion target might be a location set that represents a range or a set of ranges.

Each range corresponds to a set of information items in the acquired infoset. [Definition: An information item is said to beselected by a range if it occurs after (in document order) the starting point of the range and before the ending point of the range.]

[Definition: An information item is said to be partially selected by a range if it contains only the starting point of the range, or only the ending point of the range.] By definition, a character information item cannot be partially selected. The set of top-level included items is the union, in document order with duplicates removed, of the information items eitherselected or partially selected by the range. The children property of selected information items is not modified. The childrenproperty of partially selected information items is the set of information items that are in turn either selected or partially selected, and so on.

Point Locations

The inclusion target might be a location set that represents a point. In this case the set of included items is empty.

Element, Comment, and Processing Instruction Information Items

The inclusion target might be an element node, a comment node, or a processing instruction node, respectively representing anelement information item, a comment information item, or a processing instruction information item. In this case the set of top-level included items consists of the information item corresponding to the element, comment, or processing instruction node in theacquired infoset.

Attribute and Namespace Declaration Information Items

It is a fatal error for the inclusion target to be an attribute node or a namespace node.

Inclusion Loops

When recursively processing an xi:include element, it is a fatal error to process another xi:include element with an include location and xpointer attribute value that have already been processed in the inclusion chain.

In other words, the following are all legal:

- *An xi*: Include element may reference the document containing the include element, when parse="text".
- *An xi*: Include element may identify a different part of the same local resource (same href, different xpointer).

- *Two non-nested xi*: Include elements may identify a resource which itself contains an xi:include element.

The following are illegal:

- *An xi*: Include element pointing to itself or any ancestor thereof, when parse="xml".
- *An xi*: Include element pointing to any include element or ancestor thereof which has already been processed at a higher level.

Included Items when Parse="text"

When parse="text", the include location is dereferenced and the resource is fetched and transformed to a set of character information items. This feature facilitates the inclusion of working XML examples, as well as other text-based formats.

Resources that are unavailable for any reason (for example the resource doesn't exist, connection difficulties or security restrictions prevent it from being fetched, the URI scheme isn't a fetchable one, or the resource is in an unsupported encoding) result in a resource error.

The encoding of such a resource is determined by:

- External encoding information, if available, otherwise
- If the media type of the resource indicates, according to XML Media Types [IETF RFC 3023], that the resource is XML, for example text/xml or application/xml or matches text/*+xml or application/*+xml, then the encoding is determined as specified in [XML 1.0] or [XML 1.1] section 4.3.3, as appropriate, otherwise
- The value of the encoding attribute if one exists, otherwise
- UTF-8.

Byte sequences outside the range allowed by the encoding are a fatal error. Characters that are not permitted in XML documents also are a fatal error.

Each character obtained from the transformation of the resource is represented in the top-level included items as a character information item with the character code set to the character code in ISO 10646 encoding, and the element content whitespaceset to false. When the first character is U+FEFF and is interpreted as a Byte-Order Mark, it should be discarded. It is interpreted as a BOM in UTF-8, UTF-16, and UTF-32 encodings; it is not interpreted as a BOM in the UTF-16LE, UTF-16BE, UTF-32LE, and UTF-32BE encodings.

The [Character Model] discusses normalization of included text.

Fallback Behaviour

XInclude processors must perform fallback behaviour in the event of a resource error, as follows:

If the children of the xi: Include element information item in the source infoset contain exactly one xi:fallback element, the top-level included items consist of the information items corresponding to the result of performing XInclude processing on the childrenof the xi:fallback element. It is a fatal error if there is zero or more than one xi:fallback element.

Note: Fallback content is not dependent on the value of the parse attribute. The xi:fallback element can contain markup even when parse="text". Likewise, it can contain a simple string when parse="xml".

Creating the Result Infoset

The result infoset is a copy of the source infoset, with each xi:include element processed as follows:

The information item for the xi:include element is found. [Definition: The parent property of this item refers to an information item called the include parent.] The children property of the include parent is modified by replacing the xi:include element information item with the top-level included items. The parent property of each included item is set to the include parent.

It is a fatal error to attempt to replace an xi:include element appearing as the document (top-level) element in the source infoset with something other than a list of zero or more comments, zero or more processing instructions, and one element. Some processors may not be able to represent an element's in-scope namespaces property if it does not include bindings for all the prefixes bound in its parent's in-scope namespaces. Such processors may therefore include additional namespace bindings inherited from the include parent in the in-scope namespaces of the included items.

The inclusion history of each top-level included item is recorded in the extension property include history. The include historyproperty is a list of element information items, representing the xi:include elements for recursive levels of inclusion. If an include history property already appears on a top-level included item, the xi:include element information item is prepended to the list. If no include history property exists, then this property is added with the single value of the xi:include element information item.

The included items will all appear in the result infoset. This includes unexpanded entity reference information items if they are present.

Intra-document references within xi:include elements are resolved against the source infoset. The effect of this is that the order in which xi:include elements are processed does not affect the result.

Unparsed Entities

Any unparsed entity information item appearing in the references property of an attribute on the included items or any descendant thereof is added to the unparsed entities property of the result infoset's document information item, if it is not a duplicate of an existing member. Duplicates do not appear in the result infoset.

Unparsed entity items with the same name, system identifier, public identifier, declaration base URI, notation name, andnotation are considered to be duplicate. An application may also be able to detect that unparsed entities are duplicate through other means. For instance, the URI resulting from combining the system identifier and the declaration base URI is the same.

Notations

Any notation information item appearing in the references

property of an attribute in the included items or any descendant thereof is added to the notations property of the result infoset's document information item, if it is not a duplicate of an existing member. Likewise, any notation referenced by an unparsed entity added as described in 4.5.1 Unparsed Entities, is added unless it is a duplicate. Duplicates do not appear in the result infoset.

Notation items with the same name, system identifier, public identifier, and declaration base URI are considered to be duplicate. An application may also be able to detect that notations are duplicate through other means. For instance, the URI resulting from combining the system identifier and the declaration base URI is the same.

It is a fatal error to include notation items with the same name, but which are not determined to be duplicates.

References Property Fixup

During inclusion, an attribute information item whose attribute type property is IDREF or IDREFS has a references property with zero or more element values from the source or included infosets. These values must be adjusted to correspond to element values that occur in the result infoset. During this process, XInclude also corrects inconsistencies between the references property and the attribute type property, which might arise in the following circumstances:

- A document fragment contains an IDREF pointing to an element in the included document but outside the part being included. In this case there is no element in the result infoset that corresponds to the element value in the original referencesproperty.
- A document or document fragment is not self-contained. That is, it contains IDREFs which do not refer to an element within that document or document fragment, with the intention that these references will be realised after inclusion. In this case, the value of the references property is unknown or has no value.
- The result infoset has ID clashes–that is, more than

one attribute with attribute type ID with the same normalized value. In this case, attributes with attribute type IDREF or IDREFS with the same normalized value might have different values for their references properties.

In resolving these inconsistencies, XInclude takes the attribute type property as definitive. In the result infoset, the value of thereferences property of an attribute information item whose attribute type property is IDREF or IDREFS is adjusted as follows:

For each token in the normalized value property, the references property contains an element information item with the same properties as the element information item in the result infoset with an attribute with attribute type ID and normalized value equal to the token. The order of the elements in the references property is the same as the order of the tokens appearing in thenormalize value. If for any of the token values, no element or more than one element is found, the references property has no value.

Namespace Fixup

The in-scope namespaces property ensures that namespace scope is preserved through inclusion. However, after inclusion, thenamespace attributes property might not provide the full list of namespace declarations necessary to interpret qualified names in attribute or element content in the result. It is therefore not recommended that XInclude processors expose namespace attributesin the result. If this is unavoidable, the implementation may add attribute information items to the namespace attributes property in order to approximate the information conveyed by in-scope namespaces.

Base URI Fixup

The base URI property of the acquired infoset is not changed as a result of merging the infoset, and remains unchanged after merging. Thus relative URI references in the included infoset resolve to the same URI despite being included into a document with a potentially different base URI in effect. xml:base attributes are added to the result infoset to indicate this fact.

Each element information item in the top-level included items which has a different base URI than its include parent has anattribute information item added to its attributes property.

This attribute has the following properties:

- A namespace name of namespace.
- A local name of base.
- A prefix of xml.
- A normalized value equal to either the base URI of the element, or an equivalent URI reference relative to the base URI of the include parent. The circumstances in which a relative URI is desirable, and how to compute such a relative URI, are implementation-dependent.
- A specified flag indicating that this attribute was actually specified in the start-tag of its element.
- An attribute type of CDATA.
- A references property with no value.
- An owner element of the information item of the element.

If an xml:base attribute information item is already present, it is replaced by the new attribute.

Language Fixup

While the xml: lang attribute is described as inherited by XML, the XML Information Set makes no provision for preserving the inheritance of this property through document composition such as XInclude provides. This section introduces a languageproperty which records the scope of xml:lang information in order to preserve it during inclusion.

An XInclude processor should augment the source infoset and the acquired infoset by adding the language property to eachelement information item. The value of this property is the normalized value of the xml:lang attribute appearing on that element if one exists, with xml:lang="" resulting in no value, otherwise it is the value of the language property of the element's parent element if one exists, otherwise the property has no value.

Each element information item in the top-level included items which has a different value of language than its include parent(taking case-insensitivity into account per [IETF RFC 3066]), or that has a value if its include parent is a document information item, has an attribute information item added to its attributes property.

This attribute has the following properties:

- A namespace name of http://www.w3.org/XML/1998/namespace.
- A local name of lang.
- A prefix of xml.
- A normalized value equal to the language property of the element. If the language property has no value, the normalized value is the empty string.
- A specified flag indicating that this attribute was actually specified in the start-tag of its element.
- An attribute type of CDATA.
- A references property with no value.
- An owner element of the information item of the element.

If an xml:lang attribute information item is already present, it is replaced by the new attribute.

Note: The xml:space attribute is not treated specially by XInclude.

Properties Preserved by the Infoset

As an infoset transformation, XInclude operates on the logical structure of XML documents, not on their text serialization. All properties of an information item described in [XML Information Set] other than those specifically modified by this specification are preserved during inclusion. The include history and language properties introduced in this specification is also preserved. Extension properties such as [XML Schemas] Post Schema Validation Infoset (PSVI) properties are discarded by default. However, an XInclude processor may, at user option, preserve these properties in the resulting infoset if they are correct according to the specification describing the semantics of the extension properties.

For instance, the PSVI validity property describes the conditions of ancestors and descendants. Modification of ancestors and descendants during the XInclude process can render the value of this property inaccurate. By default, XInclude strips this property, but by user option the property could be recalculated to obtain a semantically accurate value. Precisely how this is accomplished is outside the scope of this specification.

CONFORMANCE

Markup Conformance

An element information item conforms to this specification if it meets the structural requirements for include elements defined in this specification. This specification imposes no particular constraints on DTDs or XML schemas; conformance applies only to elements and attributes.

Application Conformance

An application conforms to XInclude if it:

- Supports [XML 1.0] and [Namespaces in XML] or [XML 1.1] and [Namespaces in XML 1.1], the [XML Information Set], [XML Base], the [XPointer Framework], and the [XPointer element() scheme];
- Stops processing when a fatal error is encountered;
- Observes the mandatory conditions (must) set forth in this specification, and for any optional conditions (should and may) it chooses to observe, observes them in the way prescribed; and
- Performs markup conformance testing according to all the conformance constraints appearing in this specification.

Support for the [XPointer xpointer() Scheme] is not mandatory for full XInclude conformance. Authors are advised that use of xpointer() and other XPointer schemes than element() might not be supported by all conformant XInclude implementations.

XML Information Set Conformance

This specification conforms to the [XML Information Set].

The following information items must be present in the input infosets to enable correct processing:

- Document information items with children and base URI properties.
- Element information items with namespace name, local name, children, attributes, base URI and parent properties.
- Attribute information items with namespace name, local name and normalized value properties.

Additionally, XInclude processing might generate the following kinds of information items in the result:

- Character information items with character code, element content whitespace and parent properties.

XInclude extends the infoset with the property include history, which may appear on the following types of information items in the result:

- Element information items.
- Processing instruction information items.
- Comment information items.
- Character information items.

XInclude also extends the infoset with the property language, which may appear on element information items in the result.

XML BASE

INTRODUCTION

The XML Linking Language [XLink] defines Extensible Markup Language (XML) 1.0 [XML] constructs to describe links between resources. One of the stated requirements on XLink is to support HTML [HTML 4.01] linking constructs in a generic way. The HTML BASE element is one such construct which the XLink Working Group has considered. BASE allows authors to explicitly specify a document's base URI for the purpose of resolving relative URIs in links to external images, applets, form-processing programmes, style sheets, and so on.

This document describes a mechanism for providing base URI services to XLink, but as a modular specification so that other XML applications benefiting from additional control over relative URIs but not built upon XLink can also make use of it. The syntax consists of a single XML attribute named xml:base.

The deployment of XML Base is through normative reference by new specifications, for example XLink and the XML Infoset. Applications and specifications built upon these new technologies will natively support XML Base. The behaviour of xml:baseattributes in applications based on specifications that do not have direct or indirect normative reference to XML Base is undefined.

This specification does not attempt to specify which text strings in a document are to be interpreted as URIs. That is the responsibility of each XML vocabulary. The question addressed by this specification is: given a relative URI in an XML document, what base URI is it resolved against?

It is expected that a future RFC for XML Media Types will specify XML Base as the mechanism for establishing base URIs in the media types it defines.

TERMINOLOGY

[*Definition*: The key words must, must not, required, shall, shall not, should, should not, recommended, may, andoptional in this specification are to be interpreted as described in [RFC 2119].]

The terms base URI and relative URI are used in this specification as they are defined in [RFC 3986].

3 XML:BASE ATTRIBUTE

The attribute xml:base may be inserted in XML documents to specify a base URI other than the base URI of the document or external entity. The value of this attribute is interpreted as a Legacy Extended IRI (LEIRI) as defined in the W3C Note"Legacy extended IRIs for XML resource identification" [LEIRI]. In namespace-aware XML processors, the"xml" prefix is bound to the namespace name as described in Namespaces in XML [XML Names]. Note that xml:base can be still used by non-namespace-aware processors.

URI REFERENCE ENCODING AND ESCAPING

The value of an xml:base attribute is a Legacy Extended IRI (LEIRI) and may contain characters not allowed in URIs. (However, some characters allowed in LEIRIs are not legal XML characters, and cannot therefore appear in xml:base values.)

In accordance with the principle that per cent-encoding must occur as late as possible in the processing chain, applications which provide access to the base URI of an element should calculate and return the value without escaping.

RESOLVING RELATIVE URIS

Relation to RFC 3986

RFC 3986 [RFC 3986] provides for base URI information to be embedded within a document.

The rules for determining the base URI can be summarized as follows (highest priority to lowest:

- The base URI is embedded in the document's content.
- The base URI is that of the encapsulating entity (message, document, or none).
- The base URI is the URI used to retrieve the entity.
- The base URI is defined by the context of the application.

Note: The term"entity" in points #2 and #3 above uses the RFC 3986 meaning of the term. Elsewhere in this document the term"entity" is used in the XML sense.

This document specifies the details of rule #1 for embedding base URI information in the specific case of XML documents.

Granularity of Base URI Information

Relative URIs appearing in an XML document are always resolved relative to either an element, a document entity, or an external entity. There is no provision for finer granularity, such as per-attribute, per-character, or per-entity base information. Neither internal entities, whether declared in the internal subset or in an external DTD, nor freestanding text (text not enclosed in an element) in an external entity, are considered to set a base URI separate from the base URI in scope for the entity reference.

The base URI of a document entity or an external entity is determined by RFC 3986 rules, namely, that the base URI is the URI used to retrieve the document entity or external entity.

The base URI of an element is:

- The base URI specified by an xml:base attribute on the element, if one exists, otherwise
- The base URI of the element's parent element within the document entity or external entity, if one exists, otherwise
- The base URI of the document entity or external entity containing the element.

Note: It follows that the base URI specified by an xml:base attribute is inherited by descendant elements within the same entity until another element with an xml:base attribute is encountered.

The base URI of an element bearing an xml:base attribute with a value that is not a valid Legacy Extended IRI is application dependent.

Matching URIs with Base URIs

The base URI corresponding to a given relative URI appearing in an XML document is determined as follows:

- The base URI for a URI reference appearing in text content is the base URI of the element containing the text.
- The base URI for a URI reference appearing in an xml:base attribute is the base URI of the parent element of the element bearing the xml:base attribute,

if one exists within the document entity or external entity, otherwise the base URI of the document entity or external entity containing the element.

- The base URI for a URI reference appearing in any other attribute value, including default attribute values, is the base URI of the element bearing the attribute.
- The base URI for a URI reference appearing in the content of a processing instruction is the base URI of the parent element of the processing instruction, if one exists within the document entity or external entity, otherwise the base URI of the document entity or external entity containing the processing instruction.

Note: The presence of xml:base attributes might lead to unexpected results in the case where the attribute value is provided, not directly in the XML document entity, but via a default attribute. For instance, such a declaration in an external entity might not be read by software which is based on a non-validating XML processor. Defaulting attributes through an external mechanism such as XML Schema may also lead to unexpected results; even if a validating processor is used by the application, the addition of defaulted attributes subsequent to creation of the infoset can cause xml:base attributes to get out of sync with the [base URI] infoset property. For these reasons, xml:base values should be provided either directly in the XML document instance or via default attributes declared in the internal subset of the DTD.

Interpretation of Same-Document References

RFC 3986 defines certain relative URI references, in particular the empty string and those of the form #fragment, as same-document references. Dereferencing of same-document references is handled specially. However, their use as the value of anxml:base attribute does not involve dereferencing, and XML Base processors should resolve them in the usual way. In particular,xml:base="" does not reset the base URI to that of the containing document.

Note: Some existing processors do treat these xml:base values as resetting the base URI to that of the containing document, so the use of such values is strongly discouraged.

- The published errata have been incorporated;
- The definition of URI reference has been switched from RFC2396 to 3986;
- The xml:base attribute has been redescribed as a Legacy Extended IRI, but this does not change its syntax (the December 2006 PER used the term"XML Resource Identifier" which was to be defined in an XLink revision, but that plan has been superseded by the definition of LEIRI in the W3C Note);
- Implementations are now encouraged to return base"URIs" without escaping non-URI characters;
- The meanings of xml:base="" and xml:base="#frag" have been clarified;
- The expected reference to XML Base in the forthcoming XML Media Types RFC ("son of 3023") has been noted;
- It has been clarified that normal validity rules apply to the xml:base attribute;
- The out-of-date appendix describing effects on other standards has been removed;
- Various minor editorial changes have been made.

5

XML Schema

OVERVIEW

SCHEMAS AND SCHEMA LANGUAGES

A schema is a definition of the syntax of an XML-based language (*i.e.*, it defines a class of XML documents). A schema language is a formal language for expressing schemas.

Schema processing: Given an XML document and a schema, a schema processor,

- Checks for validity, *i.e.* that the document conforms to the schema requirements
- If the document is valid, a normalized version is output: default attributes and elements are inserted, parsing information may be added, etc.

CHOOSING A SCHEMA LANGUAGE

There have been many schema language proposals.

W3C proposals:

- DTD
- XML-Data, January 1998
- DCD (Document Content Description), July 1998
- DDML (Document Definition Markup Language), January 1999
- SOX (Schema for Object-oriented XML), July 1999
- XML Schema

Non-W3C proposals:

- Assertion Grammars by Dave Raggett
- Schematron by Rick Jellife

- TREX (Tree Regular Expressions for XML) by James Clark
- Examplotron by Eric van der Vlist
- RELAX by Makoto Murara/ RELAX NG by Murata and Clark
- DSD (Document Structure Description),

Unlike for many other XML technologies, it has proved difficult to reach a consensus–probably because:

- It is an inherently difficult problem
- People have different needs from a schema language
- The official (W3C) proposals are not very good however, most schema languages have many similarities.

We shall look at W3C's DTD and XML Schema proposals and at the DSD proposal developed by BRICS and AT&T.

XML-DATA

Schemas define the characteristics of classes of objects. This paper describes an XML vocabulary for schemas, that is, for defining and documenting object classes. It can be used for classes which as strictly syntactic (for example, XML) or those which indicate concepts and relations among concepts (as used in relational databases, KR graphs and RDF). The former are called"syntactic schemas;" the latter"conceptual schemas."

For example, an XML document might contain a"book" element which lexically contains an"author" element and a"title" element. An XML-Data schema can describe such syntax. However, in another context, we may simply want to represent more abstractly that books have titles and authors, irrespective of any syntax. XML-Data schemas can describe such conceptual relationships. Further, the information about books, titles and authors might be stored in a relational database, in which XML-Data schemas describe row types and key relationships.

One immediate implication of the ideas in this paper is that XML document types can now be described using XML itself, rather than DTD systax. Another is that XML-Data schemas provide a common vocabulary for ideas which overlap between syntactic, database and conceptual schemas. All features can be used together as appropriate.

Schemas are composed principally of declarations for:

- Concepts
- Classes of objects
  - Class hierarchies
  - Properties
  - Constraints
  - Relationships
  - Indicated by primary key to foreign key matching
  - Indicated by URI
- XML DTD Grammars and Compatibility
  - grammatical rules governing the valid nesting of the elements and attributes
  - attributes of elements
  - internal and external entities, represented by intEntityDecl and extEntityDecl
  - notations, represented by notationDcl
- Datatypes giving parsing rules and implementation formats.
- Mapping rules allowing abbreviated grammars to map to a conceptual data model.

The Schema Element Type

All schema declarations are contained within a schema element, like this:

```
<?XML version='1.0' ?>
<?xml:namespace name="urn:uuid:BDC6E3F0-6DA3-11d1-
A2A3-00AA00C14882/" as="s"/?>
<s:schema id='ExampleSchema'>
  <!-- schema goes here. -->
</s:schema>
```

The namespace of the vocabulary described in this document is named"urn:uuid:BDC6E3F0-6DA3-11d1-A2A3-00AA00C14882/".

The ElementType Declaration

The heart of an XML-Data schema is the elementType declaration, which defines a class of objects (or"type of element" in XML terminology). The id attribute serves a dual role of identifying the definition, and also naming the specific class.

```
<elementType id="author"/>
```

Within an elementType, the description subelement may be used to provide a human-readable description of the element's purpose.

```
<elementType id="author">
 <description>The person, natural or otherwise,
who wrote the book.</description>
</elementType >
```

Properties and Content Models

Subelements within elementType define characteristics of the class's members.

An XML"content model" is a description of the contents that may validly appear within a particular element type in a document instance.

```
<elementType id="author">
   <string/>
</elementType>
<elementType id="Book">
   <element type="#author" occurs="ONEORMORE"/>
</elementType>
```

The example above defines two elements, author and book, and says that a book has one or more authors. The author element may contain a string of character data (but no other elements). For example, the following is valid:

```
<Book>
  <author>Henry Ford</author>
  <author>Samuel Crowther</author>
</Book>
```

Within an elementType, various specialized subelements (element, group, any, empty, string etc.) indicate which subelements (properties) are allowed/required. Ordinarily, these imply not only the cardinality of the subelements but also their sequence. (We discuss a means to relax sequence later.)

Element

Element indicates the containment of a single element type (property). Each element contains an href attribute referencing another elementType, thereby including it in the content model syntacticly, or declaring it to be a property of the object class conceptually. The element may be required or optional, and may occur multiple times, as indicated by its occurs attribute having one of the four values "Required", "Optional", "Zeroormore" or"Onemore". It has a default of"Required".

```
<elementType id="Book">
   <element type="#title" occurs="OPTIONAL"/>
   <element type="#author" occurs="ONEORMORE"/>
</elementType>
```

The example above describes a book element type. Here, each instance of a book may contain a title, and must contain one or more authors.

```
<Book>
  <author>Henry Ford</author>
  <author>Samuel Crowther</author>
  <title>My Life and Work</title>
</Book>
```

When we discuss type hierarchies, later, we will see that an element type may have subtypes. If so, inclusion of an element type in a content model permits elements of that type directly and all its subtypes.

Open and Closed Content Models

XML typically does not allow an element to contain content unless that content was listed in the model. This is useful in some cases, but overly in others in which we would like the listed content model to govern the cardinality and other aspects of whichever subelements are explicitly named, while allowing that other subelements can appear in instances as well.

The distinction is effected by the content attribute taking the values"OPEN" and"CLOSED." The default is"OPEN" meaning that all element types not explicitly listed are valid, without order restrictions. (This idea has a close relation to the Java concept of a final class.)

For example, the following instance data for a book, including the unmentioned element copyrightDate would be valid given the content models declared so far, because they have all been open.

```
<Book>
  <author>Henry Ford</author>
  <author>Samuel Crowther</author>
  <title>My Life and Work</title>
  <copyrightDate>1922</copyrightDate>
</Book>
```

However, had the content model been declared closed, as follows, the copyrightDate element would be invalid.

```
<elementType id="Book" content="CLOSED">
  <element type="#title"/>
  <element type="#author" occurs="ONEORMORE"/>
  <group groupOrder="SEQ" occurs="OPTIONAL">
     <element type="#preface"/>
     <element type="#introduction"
   occurs="REQUIRED"/>
  </group>
</elementType>
```

A closed content model does not allow instances to contain any elements or attributes beyond those explicitly listed in the elementType declaration.

Default Values

An element with occurs of Required or Optional (but not Onemore or Zeroormore) can have a default value specified.

```
<elementType id="Book">
   <element type="#title"/>
   <element type="#author" occurs="ONEORMORE"/>
   <element type="#ageGrp" occurs="OPTIONAL">
    <default>adult</default>
```

```
  </element>
</elementType>
```

The default value is implied for all element instances in which it is syntactically omitted. To indicate that the default value is the only allowed value, the presence attribute is set to"FIXED".

```
<elementType id="Book">
  <element type="#title"/>
  <element type="#author" occurs="ONEORMORE"/>
  <element type="#ageGrp" occurs="OPTIONAL"
presence="FIXED">
    <default>ADULT</default>
  </element>
</elementType>
```

Presence has values of"Implied,""Specfied,""Required," and"Fixed" with the same meanings as defined in XML DTD.

Aliases and Correlatives

ElementTypes can be know be different names in different languages or domains. The equivalence of several names is effected by the sameAs attribute, as in

```
<elementTypeEquivalent id="livre" type="#Book"/>
<elementTypeEquivalent id="auteur" type="#author"/>
```

Elements are used to represent both primary object types (nouns) and also properties, relations and so forth. Relations are often known by two names, each reflecting one direction of the relationship. For example, husband and wife, above and below, earlier and later, etc. The correlative element identifies such a pairing.

```
<elementType id="author">
  <string/>
</elementType>
<elementType id="wrote">
  <correlative type="#author"/>
  <string/>
</elementType>
```

This indicates that"wrote" is another name for the"author" relation, but from the perspective of the person, not the book. That is, the two fragments below express the same fact:

```
<Person>
  <name>Henry Ford</name>
</Person>
<Book>
  <title>My Life and Work</title>
  <author>Henry Ford</author>
</Book>
...
<Person>
  <name>Henry Ford</name>
  <wrote>My Life and Work</wrote>
</Person>
<Book>
  <title>My Life and Work</title>
</Book>
```

A correlative may be defined simply to document the alternative name for the relation. However, it may also be used within a content model where it permits instances to use the alternative name. Further it may to establish constraints on the relation, indicate key relationships, etc.

Class Hierarchies

ElementTypes can be organized into categories using the superType attribute, as in:

```
<elementType id="price">
 <string/>
</elementType>
<elementType id="ThingsI'veBoughtRecently">
 <element type="#price"/>
</elementType>
<elementType id="PencilsI'veBoughtRecently">
 <superType type="#ThingsI'veBoughtRecently"/>
 <element type="#price"/>
</elementType>
<elementType id="BooksI'veBoughtRecently">
 <superType type="#ThingsI'veBoughtRecently"/>
 <element type="#price"/>
</elementType>
```

This simply indicates that, in some fashion, PencilsI'veBoughtRecently and BooksI'veBoughtRecently are subsets of ThingsI'veBoughtRecently. It implies that every valid instance of the subset is a valid instance of the superset. The superset type must have an open content model.

There are restrictions that should be followed, based on the principle that all instances of the species (subtype) must be instances of the genus (supertype):

- The genus type must have content="open".
- It must have either no groups or only groups with groupOrder="AND" (that is, no order constraints).
- You can add new elements and attributes.
- Occurs cardinality can be decreased but not increased.
- Ranges and other constraints are cummulative, that is, all apply (though the exact effect of this depends on the semantics of the constraint type).
- Default values can be made FIXED defaults.

To indicate that the content model of the subset should inherit the content model of a superset, we use a particular kind of superType called"genus" of which only one is allowed per ElementType. This copies the content model of the referenced element type and permits addition of new elements to it. Further, sub-elements occurring in the superset type, if declared again, are replaced by the newer declarations.

```
<elementType id="Book">
   <element type="#title"/>
   <element type="#author" occurs="ONEORMORE"/>
</elementType>
<elementType id="BooksI'veBoughtRecently">
   <genus type="#Book"/>
   <superType type="#ThingsI'veBoughtRecently"/>
   <element type="#price"/>
</elementType>
```

The above has the same effect as:

```
<elementType id="Book">
   <element type="#title"/>
   <element type="#author" occurs="ONEORMORE"/>
```

```
</elementType>
<elementType id="BooksI'veBoughtRecently">
   <superType type="#Book"/>
   <superType type="#ThingsI'veBoughtRecently"/>
   <element type="#title"/>
   <element type="#author" occurs="ONEORMORE"/>
   <element type="#price"/>
</elementType>
```

Elements which are References

ElementTypes and the content model elements defined so far are sufficient to declare a tree structure of elements. However, some elements such as"author" arenot only usable on their own, they also act as references to other elements. For example,"Henry Ford" is the value of the author subelement of a bookelement."Henry Ford" is also the value of the name element in a person element, and it can be used to connect these two.

```
<Book>
   <author>Henry Ford</author>
   <author>Samuel Crowther</author>
   <title>My Life and Work</title>
</Book>
<Person><name>Henry Ford</name></Person>
<Person><name>Samuel Crowther</name></Person>
```

In this capacity, such subelement are often referred to as relations when using"knowledge representation" terminology or"keys" when using database terms. (The meaning of"relation" and"key" are slightly different, but the fact which the terms recognize is the same.)

To make such references explicit in the schema, we add declarations for keys and foreign keys:

```
<elementType id="name">
  <string/>
</elementType>
<elementType id="Person">
  <element id="p1" type="#name"/>
  <key id="k1"><keyPart href="#p1"/></key>
```

```
</elementType>
<elementType id="author">
  <string/>
  <foreignKey range="#Person" key="#kl"/>
</elementType>
<elementType id="title">
  <string/>
</elementType>
<elementType id="Book">
  <element type="#title"/>
  <element type="#author" occurs="ONEORMORE"/>
</elementType>
```

The key element within person tells us that a person can be uniquely identified by his name. The foreignKey element within the author element definition says that the contents of an author element are a foreign key indentifying a person by name.

An uninformed user agent can still display the string"Henry Ford" even if it cannot determine that is supposed to be a person. A savvy agent that reads the schema can do more. It can locate the actual person.

This is the information needed for a join in database terminology. This mechanism not only handles the typical way in which properties are expressed in databases, it also handles all cases in which the contents of an element are to be interpreted as strings from a restricted vocabulary, such as enumerations, XML nmtokens, etc.

```
<Book>
  <author>Henry Ford</author>
  <author>Samuel Crowther</author>
  <title>My Life and Work</title>
  <lccn>HD9710.U54 F58 1973</lccn>
  <dewey>629.2/092/4 B</dewey >
  <isbn>0405050887</isbn>
  <series>Business<series>
</Book>
```

Although not shown here, presumably lccn, dewey and isbn are declared in the schema to be foreign keys to corrresponding fields of catalog records. Series is a foreign key to a categorization of books, of which"Business" is one category.

Keys can contain URIs, as in

```
<Book>
   <author>http://SSA.gov/blab/people/Henry+Ford</
author>
   <author>http://SSA.gov/blab/people/
Samuel+Crowther</author>
   <title>My Life and Work</title>
</Book>
```

This is indicated in the schema by a datatype of"URI":

```
<elementType id="author">
  <string/>
  <datatype dt="uri"/>
</elementType>
```

One-to-Many Relations

Element relations are binary. That is, we never express an n-to-1 relationship directly. We do not, for example, list within books a single relation that somehow resolves to all the authors. Instead, we always write the relationship on the 1-to-n side, but allow multiple occurrances of the subelement, for example, allowingbooks to have multiple occurrences of author.

```
<Person><name>Henry Ford</name></Person>
<Person><name>Samuel Crowther</name></Person>
<Person><name>Harvey S. Firestone</name></Person>
<Book>
   <author>Henry Ford</author>
   <author>Samuel Crowther</author>
   <title>My Life and Work</title>
</Book>
<Book>
   <author>Harvey S. Firestone</author>
   <author>Samuel Crowther</author>
   <title>Men and Rubber</title>
</Book>
```

This example shows a book with several persons as author, and also a person who is author of several books. We discussed such many-to-many relations more under the topic of correlations.

Multipart Keys

When the foreignKey element does not have foreignKeyPart sub-elements (as it does not above) then the entirety of the element's contents (*e.g.*"Henry Ford") should be used as the key value. However, for multipart foreign keys, or cases where the element has several sub-elements, foreignKeyPart is used, as shown below.

```
<elementType id="firstName">
  <string/>
</elementType>
<elementType id="lastName">
  <string/>
</elementType>
<elementType id="Person">
  <element id="pp1" type="#firstName"/>
  <element id="pp2" type="#lastName"/>
  <key id="k1">
   <keyPart href="#pp1"/>
   <keyPart href="#pp2"/>
  </key>
</elementType>
  <elementType id="author">
  <element id="ap1" type="#firstName"/>
  <element id="ap2" type="#lastName"/>
  <domain type="#Book"/>
  <range type="#Person"/>
  <foreignKey range="#Person" key="#k1">
   <foreignKeyPart href="#ap1"/>
   <foreignKeyPart href="#ap2"/>
  </foreignKey>
</elementType>
...
<Book>
  <title>My Life and Work</title>
  <author>
```

```
    <firstName>Henry</firstName>
    <lastName>Ford</lastName>
  </author>
</Book>
```

Attributes as References

An alternative way to express a reference is with an attribute.

```
<person id="person1"><name>Henry Ford</name></
Person>
<person id="person2"><name>Samuel Crowther</
name></Person>
<Book>
  <author name="Henry Ford"/>
  <author name="Samuel Crowther"/>
  <title>My Life and Work</title>
</Book>
```

This allows us to link a book to a person, through the author relation, using an attribute of the relation. This exactly parallels the construction we saw above under"multipart keys," where a subelement of author contained the author's name. Here, an attribute of author contains the name.

We can express this in our schema as:

```
<elementType id="author">
  <attribute name="name" id="authorname"/>
  <foreignKey range="#Person" key="#k1">
    <foreignKeyPart href="#authorname"/>
  </foreignKey>
</elementType>
```

A widely-used variant of this is to use a URI as a foreign key:

```
<Book>
  <author href="http://SSA.gov/blab/people/
Henry+Ford"/>
  <author href="http://SSA.gov/blab/people/
Samuel+Crowther"/>
  <title>My Life and Work</title>
</Book>
```

In this case, we are using the href attribute to contain a URI. This is a particular kind of foreign key, where the range is any possible resource, and where that resource is not identified by some combination of its properties but instead by a name-resolution service. We indicate this by using an attribute element, with dt="URI".

```
<elementType id="author">
  <attribute name="href" id="authorhref" dt="uri"/>
</elementType>
```

Constraints and Additional Properties

Min and Max Constraints

Elements can be limited to restricted ranges of values. The min and max elements define the lower and upper bounds.

```
<elementType id="age">
  <string/>
</elementType>
<elementType id="Person">
  <element hef="#age"><min>0</min><max>131</max></
element>
</elementType>
```

Such intervals are half-open (that is, the min value is in the interval, and the max value is the smallest value not in the interval).

This rule leads to the simplest calculation in most cases, and is unambiguous with respect to precision. In the above example, it is clear by these rules the 130.9999 is in the interval and 131 is not. However, had we said"all numbers from 0 to 130.99," in practice we would have some ambiguity regarding the status of 130.9999. Or interpretation would depend on the precision that we inferred for the original statement. The issue is particularly ambiguous for dates.

(What exactly does"From December 5 to December 8" mean? The use of half-open intervals for representation does not, however, put any requirements on how processors must display intervals. For example, dates in some contexts display differently than their storage. That is, the interval <min>1997-

12-05</min><max>1997-12-09</max> might be displayed as "December 5 through December 8".

In certain cases this rule for a half-open interval is impractical (for example, what letter follows"z" in the latin alphabet?) If so, use maxInclusive:

```
<elementType id="student">
  <element
type="#grade"><min>A</min><maxInclusive> Z</
maxInclusive></element>
</elementType>
```

Domain and Range Constraints

We can use the domain and range elements to add constraints to an element's use or value. The domain element, if present, indicates that the element may only be used as a property of certain other elements. That is, syntactically it may appear only in the content model of those other element types. It constrains the sorts of schemas that can be written with the element.

```
<elementType id="author">
  <string/>
  <domain type="#Book"/>
  <attribute name="href" dt="uri"/>
</elementType>
```

The domain property above permits author elements to be used only within elements which are either books or subsets of books. Use of domain is optional. If omitted, there is simply no restriction.

The range element is used with elements which are references and declares a restriction on the types of elements to which the relation may refer. Graphically, it describes the target end of a directed edge. Each range element references one elementType, any of which are valid. In this case, below, we have said that anauthor element must have an href attribute which is a URI reference to a Person or to an element type which is Person or a subset of Person.

```
<elementType id="author">
  <string/>
```

```
  <domain type="#Book"/>
  <attribute name="href" dt="uri" range="#Person"/>
</elementType>
```

Other useful properties

Element and attribute types can have an unlimited amount of further information added to them in the schema due to the open nature of XML with namespaces.

Using Elements from Other Schemas

A schema may use elements and attributes from other schemas in content models. For example, a subelement named"http://books.org/date" could be used within a book element as follows:

```
<?XML version='1.0' ?>
<?xml:namespace name="urn:uuid:BDC6E3F0-6DA3-11d1-
A2A3-00AA00C14882/" as="s"/?>
<s:schema>
  <elementType id="author">
     <string/>
  </elementType>
  <elementType id="title">
    <string/>
  </elementType>
  <elementType id="Book">
    <element type="#title" occurs="OPTIONAL"/>
    <element type="#author" occurs="ONEORMORE"/>
    <element href="http://books.org/date"/>
  </elementType>
</s:schema>
```

This can be abbreviated by adopting the rule that namespace-qualified names may be used within the href attribute value of an element or attribute element.

```
<?XML version='1.0' ?>
<?xml:namespace name="urn:uuid:BDC6E3F0-6DA3-11d1-
A2A3-00AA00C14882/" as="s"/?>
<?xml:namespace name=" http://books.org/" as="bk"/
?>
<s:schema>
```

```
  <elementType id="author">
   <string/>
  </elementType>
  <elementType id="title">
   <string/>
  </elementType>
  <elementType id="Book">
   <element type="#title" occurs="OPTIONAL"/>
   <element type="#author" occurs="ONEORMORE"/>
   <element href="bk:date"/>
  </elementType>
</s:schema>
```

XML-Specific Elements

Attributes

XML-Data schemas contain a number of facilities to match features of XML DTDs or to support certain characteristics of XML. The XML syntax allows that certain properties can be expressed in a form called"attributes." To support this, an elementType can contain attribute declarations, which are divided into attributes with enumerated or notation values, and all other kinds.

An attribute may be given a default value. Whether it is required or optional is signaled by presence. (Presence ordinarily defaults to implied, but if omitted and there is an explicit default, presence is set to the specified.) See the DTD at the end of this document for syntactic details.

Attributes with enumerated (and notation) values permit a values attribute, a space-separated list of legal values. The values attribute is required when the atttype is enumeration or notation, else it is forbidden. In these cases, if a default is specified, it must be one of the specified values.

```
<elementType id="Book">
  <element type="#title"/>
  <element type="#author" occurs="ONEORMORE"/>
  <attribute name="copyright"/>
  <attribute name="ageGrp" atttype="ENUMERATION"
```

```
values="child adult" default="adult"/>
</elementType>
```

describes an instance such as,

```
<book copyright="1922" ageGrp="adult">
 <title>My Life and Work</title>
 <author>
  <firstName>Henry</firstName>
  <lastName>Ford</lastName>
 </author>
</Book>
```

Attributes may also reference elementTypes, meaning that one may use the element type but with attribute syntax. This allows an attribute to explicitly have the same name and semantics even when used on different element types. There are of course some limits: The attribute can still occur only once in an instance, and it cannot contain other elements. However, this allows the semantics of the element type to be employed in attribute syntax.

```
<elementType id="Book">
 <attribute href="bk:title"/>
 <attribute href="bk:author"/>
 <attribute name="copyright"/>
 <attribute name="ageGrp" type="ENUMERATION"
values="children adult" default="adult"/>
</elementType>
```

describes an instance such as,

```
<book bk:author="Henry Ford" bk:title="My Life
and Work" ageGrp="adult"/>
```

The Internal and External Entity Declaration Element Type: IntEntityDcl and extEntityDcl

This and the next two declarations cover entities. Entities are a shorthand mechanism, similar to macros in a programming language.

```
<intEntityDcl name="LTG">
    Language Technology Group
</intEntityDcl>
<extEntityDcl name="dilbert" notation="#gif"
```

```
systemId="http://www.ltg.ed.ac.uk/~ht/dilb.gif"/>
```

Here as elsewhere, following XML, systemId must be a URI, absolute or relative, and publicId, if present, must be a Public Identifier (as defined in ISO/IEC 9070:1991, Information technology -- SGML support facilities -- Registration procedures for public text owner identifiers). If a notation is given, it must be declared (see below) and the entity will be treated as binary, *i.e.*, not substituted directly in place of references.

```
<notationDcl name="gif" systemId='http://
who.knows.where/'/>
```

The External Declarations Element Type: ExtDcls

Although we allow an external entity with declarations to be included, we recommend a different declaration for schema modularization. The extDcls declaration gives a clean mechanism for importing (fragments of) other schemas. It replaces the common SGML idiom of declaring an external parameter entity and then immediately referring to it, and has the same import, namely, that the text referred to by the combination of systemId and publicId is included in the schema in place of the extDcls element, and that replacement text is then subject to the same validity constraints and interpretation as the rest of the schema.

Note that in many cases the desired effect may be better represented by referencing elements (and attributes) from the other schema or subclassing from them.

Datatypes

A dataype indicates that the contents of an element can be interpreted as both a string and also, more specifically, as an object that can be interpreteted more specifically as a number, date, etc. The datatype indicates that the element's contents can be parsed or interpreted to yeild an object more specific than a string.

That is, we distinguish the"type" of an element from its"datatype." The former gives the semantic meaning of an element, such as"birthday" indicating the date on which someone was born. The"datatype" represents the parser class needed to decode the element's contents into an object type more specific than"string." For example,"19541022" is the 22nd of October, 1954 in ISO 8601 date format. (That is, ISO 8601 parsing rules will decode"19541022" into a date, which can then be stored as a date rather than a string.

For example, we would like an XML author to be able to say that the contents of a"size" element is an integer, meaning that it should be parsed according to numeric parsing rules and that it can be stored in integer format. In some contexts an API can expose it as an integer rather than a string.

```
<item>
  <name>shirt</name>
  <size>8</size>
</item>
```

There are two main contexts for datatypes. First, when dealing with database APIs, such as ODBC, all elements with the same name typically contain the same type of contents. For example, all sizes contain integers or all birthdays contain dates. We will return to this case shortly.

Second, and by contrast, the type of the content may vary widely from instance to instance. The softer we make our software, the more often these flexible cases occur. For example, size could contain the integer 8, or the word"small" or even a formula for computing the size.

We expose the datatype of an element instance by use of a dt:dt attribute, where the value of the attribute is a URI giving the datatype. (The URI might be explicitly in URI format or might rely on the XML namespace facility for resolution.) For example, we might find a document containing something like:

```
<?namespace name="urn:uuid:C2F41010-65B3-11d1-
A29F-00AA00C14882/" as="dt"?>
<?namespace name="http://zoosports.com/dt?"
as="zoo"?>
<purchases>
  <item>
   <name>shirt</name>
   <size dt:dt="int">8</size>
```

```
  </item>
  <item>
   <name>shoes</name>
   <size>large</size>
  </item>
  <item>
   <name>suit</name>
   <size dt:dt="zoo:script">
    =(shirtsize*1.05) + 3
   </size>
  </item>
</purchases>
```

Clearly this technique works for the heterogeneous typing in the above example. It also works for the database case where all element's of the same type have the same datatype.

```
<item> <name>shirt</name> <size dt:dt="int">8</
size> </item>
<item> <name>shoes</name> <size dt:dt="int">6</
size> </item>
<item> <name>suit</name> <size dt:dt="int">12</
size> </item>
```

As written above, this is inefficient. Fortunately, XML allows us in schemasto put attributes with default or fixed values, so we could say once that all sizeelements have a datatype with value"int". Having done so, our our instance just looks like:

```
<item> <name>shirt</name> <size>14</size> </item>
<item> <name>shoes</name> <size>6</size> </item>
<item> <name>suit</name> <size>16</size> </item>
```

In a DTD, we can set a fixed attribute value, so that all size elements have datatype"int" or we can set it as a default attribute value so that it is an integer except where explicitly noted otherwise.

```
<item> <name>shirt</name> <size>14</size> </item>
<item><name>shoes</name><size dt:dt="string">
large</size> </item>
<item> <name>suit</name> <size>16</size> </item>
```

XML DTDs today allow such attributes. For example, a

DTD can say that all shirt elements have integer datatype by the following:

```
<!ELEMENT size PCDATA >
<!ATTLIST size dt:dt"int" #FIXED >
```

XML-Data schemas allow the equivalent, though with specialized syntax:

```
<elementType id="size" >
 <datatype dt="int"/>
</elementType>
```

Elements use datatype subelements to give the datatype so that an optional presence attribute of the datatype element can indicate whether the datatype isfixed or merely a default. Attributes can also have datatypes. Because there is no possibility of their being anything other than a fixed type, the datatype of an attribute is signalled by a dt attribute:

```
<attribute id="size" dt="int"/>
```

How Typed Data is Exposed in the API

Different APIs to typed data will use the datatype attribute differently. The basic XML parser API should expose all element contents as strings regardless of any datatype attribute. (It might also contain supplementary methods to read values as more specific types such as"integer," thereby getting more efficiency.) An ODBC interface could use the datatype attribute to expose each type of element as a column, with the column's datatype determined by the element type's datatype.

Complex Data Types

If a datatype requires a complex structure for storage, or an object-based storage, this is also handled by the dt:dt attribute, where the datatype's storage format can be a structure, Java class, COM++ class, etc. For example, if an application needed to have an element stored in a"ScheduleItem" structure and using some private format, it could note this like

```
<whendt:dt="zoo:ScheduleItem">M*D1W4B19971022;
100</when>
```

The datatype does not require a private format. It could also use subelements and attributes such as,

```
<when dt:dt="zoo:ScheduleItem2">
  <month>*</month>
  <day>1</day>
  <week>4</week>
  <begin>19971022</begin>
  <recurs>100</recurs>
</when>
```

In the case of the graph-oriented interfaces (*e.g.* XML/RDF) the mapping from the XML tree to a graph should add a wrapping node for each non-string data type. The datatype property gives the type of that node. For example, the following two are graphically equivalent:

```
<size dt:dt="int">8</size>
<size><dt:int>8</dt:int></size>
```

Versioning of Instances

Adding an attribute to an element does not change the other attributes or pose any special versioning problems. For example, an application written to expect an instance to contain"<birthday>19541022</birthday>" is not harmed if the schema reveals that this is ISO 8601 format. Versioning within datatypes should be handled by the author's making sure that that subtypes of datatypes retain all the characteristics of the supertype.

If a down-level application is given a datatype it cannot process, it should expose the element contents as a supertype of the indicated datatype. In practice, this will usually mean that unrecognized datatypes will be the same as"dt:string". However, there are cases in which a type will be promoted, for example exposing a boolean in a byte or word rather than a bit, exposing a floating point number in a language's native format, etc.

The Datatypes Namespace

The datatype attribute"dt" is defined in the namespace named"urn:uuid:C2F41010-65B3-11d1-A29F-00AA00C14882/".

(See the XML Namespaces Note at the W3C site for details of namespaces.) The full URN of the attribute is"urn:uuid: C2F41010-65B3-11d1-A29F-00AA00C14882/dt".

You will have noticed that the value of the attribute, as used in the examples above, is not lexically a full URI. For example, it reads"int" or"string" etc. Datatype attribute values are abbreviated according to the following rule: If it does not contain a colon, it is a datatype defined in the datatypes namespace"urn:uuid:C2F41010-65B3-11d1-A29F-00AA00C14882/". If it contains a colon, it is to be expanded to a full URI according to the same rules used for other names, as defined by the XML Namespaces Note. For example

```
<?namespace name="urn:uuid:C2F41010-65B3-11d1-
A29F-00AA00C14882/" as="dt"?>
<?namespace name="http://zoosports.com/dt?"
as="zoo"?>
<item>
  <size dt:dt="int">8</size>
  <name dt:dt="zoo:clothing">shirt</name>
</item>
```

has two datatypes whose full names are"urn: uuid:C2F41010-65B3-11d1-A29F-00AA00C14882/integer" and"http://zoosports.com/dt?clothing".

What a Datatype's URI Means

Datatypes are identified by URIs. The URI as simply a reference to a section of a document that defines the appropriate parser and storage format of the element. To make this broadly useful, this document defines a set of common data types including all common forms of dates, plus all basic datatypes commonly used in SQL, C, C++, Java and COM (including strings).

The best form of such a document is that it should itself be an XML-Data schema where each datatype is an element declaration. For this purpose we define a<Syntax> subelement which can be used in lieu of a content model. We also define an <objecttype> subelement. Each has a URI as its value. This integrates data types with element types in general.

```
<schema:elementType id="int">
  <syntax href="urn:uuid:C2F41010-65B3-11d1-A29F-
00AA00C14882/num_to_int"/>
  <objectType href="urn:uuid:C2F41010-65B3-11d1-
A29F-00AA00C14882/integer32"/>
</schema:elementType>
<schema:elementType id="date.iso8601">
  <syntax href="urn:uuid:C2F41010-65B3-11d1-A29F-
00AA00C14882/date.iso8601_to_int32"/>
  <objecttype href="urn:uuid:C2F41010-65B3-11d1-
A29F-00AA00C14882/integer32"/>
</schema:elementType>
```

The objecttype sub-element can reference a structure, Java class, COM++ coClass, etc. The syntax subelement identifies a parser which can decode the element's content (and/or attributes) into the object type given the storage type URI. Input to the parser is the element object exposing all its attributes and content tree (that is, the subtree of the grove beginning with the element containing the dt attribute). The objectType attribute in particular is assumed available to the parser so that a single parser can support several objecttypes.

Having said this, all basic data types should be built into the parsers for efficiency and in order to ground the process. For these, the datatype elements serve only to formally document the storage types and parsers, and to give higher-level systems (such as RDF) a more formal basis for datatypes.

I do not currently propose that we attempt to write any universal notation for parsing rules. Certain popular kinds of formats, particularly dates, are not easily expressed in anything but natural language or code, and the parsers must be custom written code. In other words, the URIs for the basic syntax and objecttype elements probably resolve only to text descriptions.

Structured Data Type Attributes

Attributes in cannot XML have structure. I will separately propose some techniques to avoid this problem, specifically that the XML API should contain a method that treats attributes and subelements indistinguishably, and also that the content which is an element's value can be syntactically separated from content which is an element's properties.

Mapping Between Schemas

Certain uses of data emphasize syntax, others"conceptual" relations. Syntactic schemas often have fewer elements compared to explicitly conceptual ones.

Further, it is usually easier to design a schema that merely covers syntax rather than designing a well-thought-out conceptual data model.

An effect of this is that many practical schemas will not contain all the elements that a conceptual schema would, either for reasons of economy or because the initial schema was simply syntactic. But is it useful to make the implicit explicit over time so that more generic processors can make use of data.

For example, the following schema is essentially syntax:

```
<elementType id="author">
  <string/>
</elementType>
<elementType id="title">
  <string/>
</elementType>
<elementType id="Book">
  <element type="#title"/>
  <element type="#author" occurs="ONEORMORE"/>
</elementType>
```

with instances looking like this

```
<Book>
  <title>Paradise Lost</title>
  <author>Milton</author>
</Book>
```

On the other hand, a conceptual schema could look like this:

```
<elementType id="name">
  <string/>
</elementType>
<elementType id="Person">
  <element type="#name/>
</elementType>
```

```
<elementType id="creator">
  <range type="#Person/>
</elementType>
<elementType id="title">
  <string/>
</elementType>
<elementType id="Book">
  <element type="#title"/>
  <element type="#creator" occurs="ONEORMORE"/>
</elementType>
```

If fully explicit, its instances would look something like this:

```
<Person id="thing1">
  <name>Milton</Person>
</Person>
<Book>
  <title>Paradise Lost</title>
  <creator>
     <Person>
      <name>Milton</name>
     </Person>
  </creator>
</Book>
```

DTD

DEFINITION

Recall from earlier that XML 1.0 contains a built-in schema language: Document Type Definition

- <!DOCTYPE root-element [doctype-declaration...]> determines the name of the root element and contains the document type declarations
- <!ELEMENT element-name content-model> associates a content model to all elements of the given name

content models:

- *Empty*: No content is allowed
- Any: Any content is allowed
- (#PCDATA|element-name|...)*:"mixed content",

arbitrary sequence of character data and listed elements
  - Deterministic regular expression over element names: sequence of elements matching the expression
- Choice: (...|...|...)
- Sequence: (.........)
- Optional:...?
- Zero or more:...*
- One or more:...+
- <!ATTLIST element-name attr-name attr-type attr-default...> declares which attributes are allowed or required in which elements attribute types:
  - CDATA: any value is allowed (the default)
  - (value|...): enumeration of allowed values
  - ID, IDREF, IDREFS: ID attribute values must be unique (contain"element identity"), IDREF attribute values must match some ID (reference to an element)
  - ENTITY, ENTITIES, NMTOKEN, NMTOKENS, NOTATION: just forget these... (consider them deprecated) attribute defaults:
  - #REQUIRED: the attribute must be explicitly provided
  - #IMPLIED: attribute is optional, no default provided
  - "value": if not explicitly provided, this value inserted by default
  - #FIXED"value": as above, but only this value is allowed

PROBLEMS WITH DTD

Top 15 reasons for avoiding DTD:

1. Not itself using XML syntax (the SGML heritage can be very unintuitive + if using XML, DTDs could potentially themselves be syntax checked with a"meta DTD")
2. Mixed into the XML 1.0 spec (would be much less

confusing if specified separately + even non-validating processors must look at the DTD)

3. No constraints on character data (if character data is allowed, any character data is allowed)
4. Too simple attribute value models (enumerations are clearly insufficient)
5. Cannot mix character data and regexp content models (and the content models are generally hard to use for complex requirements)
6. No support for Namespaces (of course, XML 1.0 was defined before Namespaces)
7. Very limited support for modularity and reuse (the entity mechanism is too low-level)
8. No support for schema evolution, extension, or inheritance of declarations (difficult to write, maintain, and read large DTDs, and to define families of related schemas)
9. Limited white-space control (xml:space is rarely used)
10. No embedded, structured self-documentation (<!-- comments --> are not enough)
11. Content and attribute declarations cannot depend on attributes or element context (many XML languages use that, but their DTDs have to"allow too much")
12. Too simple ID attribute mechanism (no points-to requirements, uniqueness scope, etc.)
13. Only defaults for attributes, not for elements (but that would often be convenient)
14. Cannot specify"any element" or"any attribute" (useful for partial specifications and during schema development)
15. Defaults cannot be specified separate from the declarations (would be convenient to have defaults in separate modules)

XML SCHEMA

OVERVIEW

The XML 1.0 specification defines the concepts of well-formedness and validity; it is very simple to check a document for well-formedness, while validation requires more work but allows the user to define more powerful constraints on document structure. XML validity requires that a document follow the constraints expressed in its document type definition, which provides the rough equivalent of a context-free grammar for a document type.

For some uses, applications may need definitions of markup constructs more informative, or constraints on document structure tighter than, looser than, or simply different from those which can be expressed using document type definitions as defined in XML 1.0. There is also a widespread desire to allow markup constructs and constraints to be specified in an XML-based syntax, in order to allow tools for XML documents to be used on the specifications.

By charter, the XML Schema Working Group is assigned to address the following issues:

Structural schemas

Amechanism somewhat analogous to DTDs for constraining document structure (order, occurrence of elements, attributes).

Specific goals beyond DTD functionality are:

- Integration with namespaces
- Definition of incomplete constraints on the content of an element type
- Integration of structural schemas with primitive data types
- *Inheritance*: Existing mechanisms use content models to specify part-of relations. But they only specify kind-of relations implicitly or informally. Making kind-of relations explicit would make both understanding and maintenance easier

Primitive Data Typing

Integers, dates, and the like, based on experience with SQL, Java primitives, etc.; byte sequences ("binary data") also need to be considered

Conformance

The relation of schemata to XML document instances, and obligations on schema-aware processors, must be defined. The Working Group will define a process for checking to see that the constraints expressed in a schema are obeyed in a document (schema-validation); the relationship between schema-validity and validity as defined in XML 1.0 will be defined. The XML Schema work is interdependent with several other areas of W3C activity. These are listed below under Design Principles.

PURPOSE

The purpose of the XML schema language is to provide an inventory of XML markup constructs with which to write schemas. The purpose of a schema is to define and describe a class of XML documents by using these constructs to constrain and document the meaning, usage and relationships of their constituent parts: datatypes, elements and their content, attributes and their values, entities and their contents and notations.

Schema constructs may also provide for the specification of implicit information such as default values. Schemas document their own meaning, usage, and function. Thus, the XML schema language can be used to define, describe and catalogue XML vocabularies for classes of XML documents. Any application of XML can use the Schema formalism to express syntactic, structural and value constraints applicable to its document instances.

The Schema formalism will allow a useful level of constraint checking to be described and validated for a wide spectrum of XML applications. For applications which require other, arbitrary or complicated constraints, the application must perform its own additional validations.

USAGE SCENARIOS

The following usage scenarios describe XML applications that should benefit from XML schemas. They represent a wide range of activities and needs that are representative of the problem space to be addressed. They are intended to be used during the development of XML schemas as design cases that should be reviewed when critical decisions are made. These usage scenarios should also prove useful in helping non-members of the XML Schema Working Group understand the intent and goals of the project.

- *Publishing and syndication*: Distribution of information through publishing and syndication services. Involves collections of XML documents with complex relations among them. Structural schemas describe the properties of headlines, news stories, thumbnail images, cross-references, etc. Document views under control of different versions of a schema.
- *Electronic commerce transaction processing*: Libraries of schemas define business transactions within markets and between parties. A schema-aware processor is used to validate a business document, and to provide access to its information set.
- *Supervisory control and data acquisition*: The management and use of network devices involves the exchange of data and control messages. Schemas can be used by a server to ensure outgoing message validity, or by the client to allow it to determine what part of a message it understands. In multi-vendor environment, discriminates data governed by different schemas (industry-standard, vendor-specific) and know when it is safe to ignore information not understood and when an error should be raised instead; provide transparency control. Applications include media devices, security systems, plant automation, process control.
- *Traditional document authoring/editing governed by schema constraints*: One important class of application uses a schema definition to guide an author in the development of documents. A simple example might be a memo, whereas a more sophisticated example is the technical service manuals for a wide-body intercontinental aircraft. The application can ensure

that the author always knows whether to enter a date or a part-number, and might even ensure that the data entered is valid.

- *Use schema to help query formulation and optimization*: A query interface inspect XML schemas to guide a user in the formulation of queries. Any given database can emit a schema of itself to inform other systems what counts as legitimate and useful queries.
- *Open and uniform transfer of data between applications, including databases*: XML has become a widely used format for encoding data (including metadata and control data) for exchange between loosely coupled applications. Such exchange is currently hampered by the difficulty of fully describing the exchange data model in terms of XML DTDs; exchange data model versioning issues further complicate such interactions. When the exchange data model is represented by the more expressive XML Schema definitions, the task of mapping the exchange data model to and from application internal data models will be simplified.
- *Metadata Interchange*: There is growing interest in the interchange of metadata (especially for databases) and in the use of metadata registries to facilitate interoperability of database design, DBMS, query, user interface, data warehousing, and report generation tools. Examples include ISO 11179 and ANSI X3.285 data registry standards, and OMG's proposed XMI standard.

DESIGN PRINCIPLES

In the design of any language, trade-offs in the solution space are necessary. The following design principles should guide the working group in making these trade-offs. Design principles are desirable, but not fully measurable, characteristics.

The XML schema language shall be:

- More expressive than XML DTDs;

- Expressed in XML;
- Self-describing;
- Usable by a wide variety of applications that employ XML;
- Straightforwardly usable on the Internet;
- Optimized for interoperability;
- Simple enough to implement with modest design and runtime resources;
- Coordinated with relevant W3C specs (XML Information Set, Links, Namespaces, Pointers, Style and Syntax, as well as DOM, HTML, and RDF Schema).

The XML schema language specification shall:

- Be prepared quickly;
- Be precise, concise, human-readable, and illustrated with examples.

REQUIREMENTS

Structural Requirements

The XML schema language must define:

- Mechanisms for constraining document structure (namespaces, elements, attributes) and content (datatypes, entities, notations);
- Mechanisms to enable inheritance for element, attribute, and datatype definitions;
- Mechanism for URI reference to standard semantic understanding of a construct;
- Mechanism for embedded documentation;
- Mechanism for application-specific constraints and descriptions;
- Mechanisms for addressing the evolution of schemata;
- Mechanisms to enable integration of structural schemas with primitive data types.

Datatype Requirements

The XML schema language must:

- Provide for primitive data typing, including byte,

date, integer, sequence, SQL and Java primitive data types, etc.;
- Define a type system that is adequate for import/export from database systems (*e.g.*, relational, object, OLAP);
- Distinguish requirements relating to lexical data representation vs. those governing an underlying information set;
- Allow creation of user-defined datatypes, such as datatypes that are derived from existing datatypes and which may constrain certain of its properties (*e.g.*, range, precision, length, mask).

Conformance

The XML schema language must:
- Describe the responsibilities of conforming processors;
- Define the relationship between schemas and XML documents;
- Define the relationship between schema validity and XML validity;
- Define the relationship between schemas and XML DTDs, and their information sets;
- Define the relationship among schemas, namespaces, and validity;
- Define a useful XML schema for XML schemas;

XML SCHEMA

STRUCTURES

Introduction

This document sets out the structural part (XML Schema: Structures) of the XML Schema definition language. This document is primarily intended as a language definition reference. As such, although it contains a few examples, it is notprimarily designed to serve as a motivating introduction to the design and its features, or as a tutorial for new users.

Rather it presents a careful and fully explicit definition of that design, suitable for guiding implementations. For those in search of a step-by-step introduction to the design, the non-normative [XML Schema: Primer] is a much better starting point than this document.

Purpose

The purpose of XML Schema: Structures is to define the nature of XML schemas and their component parts, provide an inventory of XML markup constructs with which to represent schemas, and define the application of schemas to XML documents.

The purpose of an XML Schema: Structures schema is to define and describe a class of XML documents by using schema components to constrain and document the meaning, usage and relationships of their constituent parts: datatypes, elements and their content and attributes and their values. Schemas may also provide for the specification of additional document information, such as normalization and defaulting of attribute and element values. Schemas have facilities for self-documentation. Thus, XML Schema: Structures can be used to define, describe and catalogue XML vocabularies for classes of XML documents.

Any application that consumes well-formed XML can use the XML Schema: Structures formalism to express syntactic, structural and value constraints applicable to its document instances. The XML Schema: Structures formalism allows a useful level of constraint checking to be described and implemented for a wide spectrum of XML applications. However, the language defined by this specification does not attempt to provide all the facilities that might be needed by any application. Some applications may require constraint capabilities not expressible in this language, and so may need to perform their own additional validations.

Dependencies on Other Specifications

The definition of XML Schema: Structures depends on the following specifications: [XML-Infoset], [XML-Namespaces],

[XPath], and [XML Schemas: Datatypes]. See Required Information Set Items and Properties (normative) (§D) for a tabulation of the information items and properties specified in [XML-Infoset] which this specification requires as a precondition to schema-aware processing.

Type Definition Components

The abstract model provides two kinds of type definition component: simple and complex. This specification uses the phrase type definition in cases where no distinction need be made between simple and complex types.

Type definitions form a hierarchy with a single root. The subsections below first describe characteristics of that hierarchy, then provide an introduction to simple and complex type definitions themselves.

Type Definition Hierarchy

Except for a distinguished ur-type definition, every type definition is, by construction, either a restriction or anextension of some other type definition. The graph of these relationships forms a tree known as the Type Definition Hierarchy.

A type definition whose declarations or facets are in a one-to-one relation with those of another specified type definition, with each in turn restricting the possibilities of the one it corresponds to, is said to be a restriction. The specific restrictions might include narrowed ranges or reduced alternatives. Members of a type, A, whose definition is a restriction of the definition of another type, B, are always members of type B as well.

A complex type definition which allows element or attribute content in addition to that allowed by another specified type definition is said to be an extension.

A distinguished complex type definition, the ur-type definition, whose name is anyType in the XML Schema namespace, is present in each XML Schema, serving as the root of the type definition hierarchy for that schema. A type definition used as the basis for an extension or restriction is known as the base type definition of that definition.

Simple Type Definition

A simple type definition is a set of constraints on strings and information about the values they encode, applicable to thenormalized value of an attribute information item or of an element information item with no element children. Informally, it applies to the values of attributes and the text-only content of elements.

The mapping from lexical space to value space is unspecified for items whose type definition is the simple ur-type definition.

Accordingly this specification does not constrain processors' behaviour in areas where this mapping is implicated, for example checking such items against enumerations, constructing default attributes or elements whose declared type definition is the simple ur-type definition, checking identity constraints involving such items.

Simple types may also be defined whose members are lists of items themselves constrained by some other simple type definition, or whose membership is the union of the memberships of some other simple type definitions. Such list and union simple type definitions are also restrictions of the simple ur-type definition.

Complex Type Definition

A complex type definition is a set of attribute declarations and a content type, applicable to the [attributes] and [children] of an element information item respectively.

The content type may require the [children] to contain neither element nor character information items (that is, to be empty), to be a string which belongs to a particular simple type or to contain a sequence of element information items which conforms to a particular model group, with or without character information items as well.

Each complex type definition other than the ur-type definition is either:

- A restriction of a complex base type definition
- An extension of a simple or complex base type definition

A complex type which extends another does so by having additional content model particles at the end of the other definition's content model, or by having additional attribute declarations, or both.

Note: This specification allows only appending, and not other kinds of extensions. This decision simplifies application processing required to cast instances from derived to base type. Future versions may allow more kinds of extension, requiring more complex transformations to effect casting.

Declaration Components

There are three kinds of declaration component: element, attribute, and notation. Each is described in a section below. Also included is a discussion of element substitution groups, which is a feature provided in conjunction with element declarations.

ELEMENT DECLARATION

An element declaration is an association of a name with a type definition, either simple or complex, an (optional) default value and a (possibly empty) set of identity-constraint definitions. The association is either global or scoped to a containing complex type definition. A top-level element declaration with name'A' is broadly comparable to a pair of DTD declarations as follows, where the associated type definition fills in the ellipses:

```
<!ELEMENT A...>
<!ATTLIST A...>
```

Element declarations contribute to validation as part of model group validation, when their defaults and type components are checked against an element information item with a matching name and namespace, and by triggering identity-constraint definition validation.

Element Substitution Group

In XML 1.0, the name and content of an element must correspond exactly to the element type referenced in the corresponding content model.

Through the new mechanism of element substitution groups, XML Schemas provides a more powerful model supporting substitution of one named element for another. Any top-level element declaration can serve as the defining member, or head, for an element substitution group. Other top-level element declarations, regardless of target namespace, can be designated as members of the substitution group headed by this element. In a suitably enabled content model, a reference to the headvalidates not just the head itself, but elements corresponding to any other member of the substitution group as well.

All such members must have type definitions which are either the same as the head's type definition or restrictions or extensions of it. Therefore, although the names of elements can vary widely as new namespaces and members of the substitution group are defined, the content of member elements is strictly limited according to the type definition of the substitution group head.

Attribute Declaration

An attribute declaration is an association between a name and a simple type definition, together with occurrence information and (optionally) a default value. The association is either global, or local to its containing complex type definition. Attribute declarations contribute to validation as part of complex type definition validation, when their occurrence, defaults and type components are checked against an attribute information item with a matching name and namespace.

Notation Declaration

A notation declaration is an association between a name and an identifier for a notation. For an attribute information item to bevalid with respect to a NOTATION simple type definition, its value must have been declared with a notation declaration.

Model Group Components

The model group, particle, and wildcard components

contribute to the portion of a complex type definition that controls an element information item's content.

Model Group: A model group is a constraint in the form of a grammar fragment that applies to lists of element information items. It consists of a list of particles, *i.e.* element declarations, wildcards and model groups.

There are three varieties of model group:

1. Sequence (the element information items match the particles in sequential order);
2. Conjunction (the element information items match the particles, in any order);
3. Disjunction (the element information items match one of the particles).

Particle: A particle is a term in the grammar for element content, consisting of either an element declaration, a wildcard or a model group, together with occurrence constraints. Particles contribute to validation as part of complex type definition validation, when they allow anywhere from zero to many element information items or sequences thereof, depending on their contents and occurrence constraints.

A particle can be used in a complex type definition to constrain the validation of the [children] of an element information item; such a particle is called a content model.

Attribute Use: An attribute use plays a role similar to that of a particle, but for attribute declarations: an attribute declaration within a complex type definition is embedded within an attribute use, which specifies whether the declaration requires or merely allows its attribute, and whether it has a default or fixed value.

Wildcard: A wildcard is a special kind of particle which matches element and attribute information items dependent on their namespace name, independently of their local names.

Identity-constraint Definition Components

An identity-constraint definition is an association between a name and one of several varieties of identity-constraint related to uniqueness and reference. All the varieties use [XPath] expressions to pick out sets of information items relative to particular target element information items which are unique, or a key, or a valid reference, within a specified scope. An element information item is only valid with respect to an element declaration with identity-constraint definitions if those definitions are all satisfied for all the descendants of that element information item which they pick out.

Group Definition Components

There are two kinds of convenience definitions provided to enable the re-use of pieces of complex type definitions: model group definitions and attribute group definitions.

Model Group Definition

A model group definition is an association between a name and a model group, enabling re-use of the same model group in several complex type definitions.

Attribute Group Definition

An attribute group definition is an association between a name and a set of attribute declarations, enabling re-use of the same set in several complex type definitions.

Annotation Components

An annotation is information for human and/or mechanical consumers. The interpretation of such information is not defined in this specification.

Constraints and Validation Rules

The specification describes two kinds of constraints on XML documents: well-formedness andvalidity constraints. Informally, the well-formedness constraints are those imposed by the definition of XML itself (such as the rules for the use of the < and > characters and the rules for proper nesting of elements), while validity constraints are the further constraints on document structure provided by a particular DTD.

The preceding section focused on validation, that is the constraints on information items which schema components supply. In fact however this specification provides four different kinds of normative statements about schema components, their representations in XML and their contribution to the validation of information items:

Conformance

This specification describes three levels of conformance for schema aware processors. The first is required of all processors. Support for the other two will depend on the application environments for which the processor is intended.

[Definition:] Minimally conforming processors must completely and correctly implement the Schema Component Constraints,Validation Rules, and Schema Information Set Contributions contained in this specification.

Names and Symbol Spaces

If all such names were assigned from the same"pool", then it would be impossible to have, for example, a simple type definition and an element declaration both with the name"title" in a given target namespace.

Therefore [Definition:] this specification introduces the term symbol space to denote a collection of names, each of which is unique with respect to the others. A symbol space is similar to the non-normative concept of namespace partition introduced in[XML-Namespaces]. There is a single distinct symbol space within a given target namespace for each kind of definition and declaration component identified in XML Schema Abstract Data Model, except that within a target namespace, simple type definitions and complex type definitions share a symbol space. Within a given symbol space, names are unique, but the same name may appear in more than one symbol space without conflict. For example, the same name can appear in both a type definition and an element declaration, without conflict or necessary relation between the two.

Locally scoped attribute and element declarations are special with regard to symbol spaces. Every complex type definition defines its own local attribute and element declaration symbol spaces, where these symbol spaces are distinct from each other and from any of the other symbol spaces. So, for example, two complex type definitions having the same target namespace can contain a local attribute declaration for the unqualified name"priority", or contain a local element declaration for the name"address", without conflict or necessary relation between the two.

Schema Component Details

Introduction

The following sections provide full details on the composition of all schema components, together with their XML representations and their contributions to assessment. Each section is devoted to a single component, with separate subsections for,

- *Properties*: their values and significance
- XML representation and the mapping to properties
- Constraints on representation
- Validation rules
- Post-schema-validation infoset contributions
- Constraints on the components themselves

The sub-sections immediately below introduce conventions and terminology used throughout the component sections.

Components and Properties: Components are defined in terms of their properties, and each property in turn is defined by giving its range, that is the values it may have. This can be understood as defining a schema as a labeled directed graph, where the root is a schema, every other vertex is a schema component or a literal (string, boolean, number) and every labeled edge is a property. The graph is not acyclic: multiple copies of components with the same name in the same symbol space may not exist, so in some cases re-entrant chains of properties must exist. Equality of components for the purposes of this specification is always defined as equality of names (including target namespaces) within symbol spaces.

Throughout this specification, the term absent is used as a distinguished property value denoting absence.

Any property not identified as optional is required to be present; optional properties which are not present are taken to haveabsent as their value.

Any property identified as a having a set, subset or list value may have an empty value unless this is explicitly ruled out: this is not the same as absent. Any property value identified as a superset or subset of some set may be equal to that set, unless a proper superset or subset is explicitly called for.

XML Representations of Components

The principal purpose of XML Schema: Structures is to define a set of schema components that constrain the contents of instances and augment the information sets thereof. Although no external representation of schemas is required for this purpose, such representations will obviously be widely used. To provide for this in an appropriate and interoperable way, this specification provides a normative XML representation for schemas which makes provision for every kind of schema component.

[Definition:] A document in this form (*i.e.* a <schema> element information item) is a schema document. All the element information items in the XML representation of a schema must be in the XML Schema namespace, that is their[namespace name] must be.

Although a common way of creating the XML Infosets which are or contain schema documents will be using an XML parser, this is not required: any mechanism which constructs conformant infosets as defined is a possible starting point.

Two aspects of the XML representations of components presented in the following sections are constant across them all:

1. All of them allow attributes qualified with namespace names other than the XML Schema namespace itself: these appear as annotations in the corresponding schema component;
2. All of them allow an <annotation> as their first child, for human-readable documentation and/or machine-targeted information.

The Mapping between XML Representations and Components For each kind of schema component there is a corresponding normative XML representation. The sections below describe the correspondences between the properties of each kind of schema component on the one hand and the properties of information items in that XML representation on the other, together with constraints on that representation above and beyond those implicit in the Schema for Schemas (normative).

The language used is as if the correspondences were mappings from XML representation to schema component, but the mapping in the other direction, and therefore the correspondence in the abstract, can always be constructed therefrom.

In discussing the mapping from XML representations to schema components below, the value of a component property is often determined by the value of an attribute information item, one of the [attributes] of an element information item. Since schema documents are constrained by the Schema for Schemas (normative), there is always a simple type definition associated with any such attribute information item.

The phrase actual value is used to refer to the member of the value space of the simple type definition associated with an attribute information item which corresponds to its normalized value. This will often be a string, but may also be an integer, a boolean, a URI reference, etc. This term is also occasionally used with respect to element or attribute information items in a document being validated.

Many properties are identified below as having other schema components or sets of components as values. For the purposes of exposition, the definitions in this section assume that (unless the property is explicitly identified as optional) all such values are in fact present. When schema components are constructed from XML representations involving reference by name to other components, this assumption may be violated if one or more references cannot be resolved.

Forward reference to named definitions and declarations is allowed, both within and between schema documents. By the time the component corresponding to an XML representation which contains a forward reference is actually needed for validation an appropriately-named component may have become available to discharge the reference.

Attribute Declarations

Attribute declarations provide for:

- Local validation of attribute information item values using a simple type definition;
- Specifying default or fixed values for attribute information items.

The {name} property must match the local part of the names of attributes being validated.

The value of the attribute must conform to the supplied {type definition}.

A non-absent value of the {target namespace} property provides for validation of namespace-qualified attribute information items (which must be explicitly prefixed in the character-level form of XML documents). Absent values of {target namespace}validate unqualified (unprefixed) items.

A {scope} of global identifies attribute declarations available for use in complex type definitions throughout the schema. Locally scoped declarations are available for use only within the complex type definition identified by the {scope} property. This property isabsent in the case of declarations within attribute group definitions: their scope will be determined when they are used in the construction of complex type definitions. {value constraint} reproduces the functions of XML 1.0 default and #FIXED attribute values. default specifies that the attribute is to appear unconditionally in the post-schema-validation infoset, with the supplied value used whenever the attribute is not actually present; fixed indicates that the attribute value if present must equal the supplied constraint value, and if absent receives the supplied value as for default. Note that it is values that are supplied and/or checked, not strings.

Note: A more complete and formal presentation of the semantics of {name}, {target namespace} and {value constraint} is provided in conjunction with other aspects of complex type validation XML Representation of Attribute Declaration Schema Components The XML representation for an attribute declaration schema component is an <attribute> element information item. It specifies a simple type definition for an attribute either by reference or explicitly, and may provide default information.

Attribute declarations can appear at the top level of a schema document, or within complex type definitions, either as complete (local) declarations, or by reference to top-level declarations, or within attribute group definitions. For complete declarations, top-level or local, the type attribute is used when the declaration can use a built-in or pre-declared simple type definition. Otherwise an anonymous <simpleType> is provided inline.

The default when no simple type definition is referenced or provided is the simple ur-type definition, which imposes no constraints at all. Attribute information items validated by a top-level declaration must be qualified with the {target namespace} of that declaration (if this is absent, the item must be unqualified).

Control over whether attribute information items validated by a local declaration must be similarly qualified or not is provided by the form [attribute], whose default is provided by the attributeFormDefault[attribute] on the enclosing <schema>, via its determination of {target namespace}.

The names for top-level attribute declarations are in their own symbol space. The names of locally-scoped attribute declarations reside in symbol spaces local to the type definition which contains them.

Attribute Declaration Information Set Contributions The {name} property must match the local part of the names of element information items being validated.

A {scope} of global identifies element declarations available for use in content models throughout the schema. Locally scoped declarations are available for use only within the complex type identified by the {scope} property. This property is absent in the case of declarations within named model groups: their scope is determined when they are used in the construction of complex type definitions.

A non-absent value of the {target namespace} property provides for validation of namespace-qualified element information items. Absent values of {target namespace} validate unqualified items.

An element information item is valid if it satisfies the {type definition}. For such an item, schema information set contributions appropriate to the {type definition} are added to the corresponding element information item in the post-schema-validation infoset.

Element declarations are potential members of the substitution group, if any, identified by {substitution group affiliation}. Potential membership is transitive but not symmetric; an element declaration is a potential member of any group of which its {substitution group affiliation} is a potential member. Actual membership may be blocked by the effects of {substitution group exclusions} or{disallowed substitutions}, see below.

An empty {substitution group exclusions} allows a declaration to be nominated as the {substitution group affiliation} of other element declarations having the same {type definition} or types derived therefrom.

The explicit values of {substitution group exclusions} rule out element declarations having types which are extensions or restrictions respectively of {type definition}. If both values are specified, then the declaration may not be nominated as the {substitution group affiliation} of any other declaration.

Element Declaration Validation Rules

Validation Rule: Element Locally Valid (Element)

For an element information item to be locally valid with respect to an element declaration all of the following must be true:

- The declaration must not be absent.
- Its {abstract} must be false.
- The appropriate case among the following must be true:

If nillable is false, then there must be no attribute information item among the element information item's [attributes]whose [namespace name] is identical to and whose [local name] is nil. {nillable} is true and there is such an attribute information item and its actual value is true, then all of the following must be true:

The element information item must have no character or element information item [children].

There must be no fixed:

- If there is an attribute information item among the element information item's [attributes] whose [namespace name] is identical to and whose [local name] is type, then all of the following must be true:

Schema Component Constraint: Element Declarations Consistent If the {particles} contains, either directly, indirectly (that is, within the {particles} of a contained model group, recursively) orimplicitly two or more element declaration particles with the same {name} and {target namespace}, then all their type definitions must be the same top-level definition, that is, all of the following must be true:

- All their {type definition}s must have a non-absent {name}.
- All their {type definition}s must have the same {name}.
- All their {type definition}s must have the same {target namespace}.

[*Definition*:] A list of particles implicitly contains an element declaration if a member of the list contains that element declaration in its substitution group.

Schema Component Constraint: Unique Particle Attribution

A content model must be formed such that during validation of an element information item sequence, the particle component contained directly, indirectly or implicitly therein with which to attempt to validate each item in the sequence in turn can be uniquely determined without examining the content or attributes of that item, and without any information about the items in the remainder of the sequence.

Schema Component Constraint: Effective Total Range (All and Sequence)

The effective total range of a particle whose {term} is a group whose {compositor} is all or sequence is a pair of minimum and maximum, as follows:

Minimum: The product of the particle's {min occurs} and the sum of the {min occurs} of every wildcard or element declaration particle in the group's {particles} and the minimum part of the effective total range of each of the group particles in the group's{particles} (or 0 if there are no {particles}).

Maximum: unbounded if the {max occurs} of any wildcard or element declaration particle in the group's {particles} or the maximum part of the effective total range of any of the group particles in the group's {particles} is unbounded, or if any of those is non-zero and the {max occurs} of the particle itself is unbounded, otherwise the product of the particle's {max occurs} and the sum of the {max occurs} of every wildcard or element declaration particle in the group's {particles} and the maximum part of the effective total range of each of the group particles in the group's {particles} (or 0 if there are no {particles}). Schema Component Constraint: Effective Total Range (choice)

The effective total range of a particle whose {term} is a group whose {compositor} is choice is a pair of minimum and maximum, as follows:

Minimum: The product of the particle's {min occurs} and the minimum of the {min occurs} of every wildcard or element declaration particle in the group's {particles} and the minimum part of the effective total range of each of the group particles in the group's {particles} (or 0 if there are no {particles}).

Maximum: Unbounded if the {max occurs} of any wildcard or element declaration particle in the group's {particles} or the maximum part of the effective total range of any of the group particles in the group's {particles} is unbounded, or if any of those is non-zero and the {max occurs} of the particle itself is unbounded, otherwise the product of the particle's {max occurs} and the maximum of the {max occurs} of every wildcard or element declaration particle in the group's {particles} and the maximum part of the effective total range of each of the group particles in the group's {particles} (or 0 if there are no{particles}).

Particles

In general, multiple element information item [children], possibly with intervening character [children] if the content type is mixed, can be validated with respect to a single particle. When the {term} is an element declaration or wildcard, {min occurs} determines the minimum number of such element [children] that can occur. The number of such children must be greater than or equal to {min occurs}. If {min occurs} is 0, then occurrence of such children is optional.

Again, when the {term} is an element declaration or wildcard, the number of such element [children] must be less than or equal to any numeric specification of {max occurs}; if {max occurs} is unbounded, then there is no upper bound on the number of such children.

When the {term} is a model group, the permitted occurrence range is determined by a combination of {min occurs} and {max occurs} and the occurrence ranges of the {term}'s {particles}.

A simple type definition with an empty specification for {final} can be used as the {base type definition} for other types derived by either of extension or restriction, or as the {item type definition} in the definition of a list, or in the {member type definitions} of a union; the explicit values extension, restriction, list and union prevent further derivations by extension (to yield a complex type) and restriction (to yield a simple type) and use in constructing lists and unions respectively.

{variety} determines whether the simple type corresponds to an atomic, list or union type as defined.

As described, every simple type definition is a restriction of some other simple type (the{base type definition}), which is the simple ur-type definition if and only if the type definition in question is one of the built-in primitive datatypes, or a list or union type definition which is not itself derived by restriction from a list or union respectively. Eachatomic type is ultimately a restriction of exactly one such built-in primitive datatype, which is its {primitive type definition}.each simple type definition are selected from those defined. For atomic definitions, these are restricted to those appropriate for the corresponding {primitive type definition}. Therefore, the value space and lexical space (*i.e.* what is validated by any atomic simple type) is determined by the pair ({primitive type definition}, {facets}).

As specified in [XML Schemas: Datatypes], list simple type definitions validate space separated tokens, each of which conforms to a specified simple type definition, the {item type definition}. The item type specified must not itself be a list type, and must be one of the types identified in [XML Schemas: Datatypes] as a suitable item type for a list simple type. In this case the {facets}apply to the list itself, and are restricted to those appropriate for lists.

A union simple type definition validates strings which satisfy at least one of its {member type definitions}. As in the case of list, the {facets} apply to the union itself, and are restricted to those appropriate for unions.

The simple ur-type definition must not be named as the base type definition of any user-defined atomic simple type definitions: as it has no constraining facets, this would be incoherent.

Two particles may validate adjacent information items if they are separated by at most epsilon transitions in the most obvious transcription of a content model into a finite-state automaton.

A precise formulation of this constraint can also be offered in terms of operations on finite-state automaton: transcribe the content model into an automaton in the usual way using epsilon transitions for optionality and unbounded maxOccurs, unfolding other numeric occurrence ranges and treating the heads of substitution groups as if they were choices over all elements in the group,but using not element QNames as transition labels, but rather pairs of element QNames and positions in the model. Determinize this automaton, treating wildcard transitions as opaque. Now replace all QName+ position transition labels with the element QNames alone. If the result has any states with two or more identical-QName-labeled transitions from it, or a QName-labeled transition and a wildcard transition which subsumes it, or two wildcard transitions whose intentional intersection is non-empty, the model does not satisfy the Unique Attribution constraint.

The editors acknowledge the members of the XML Schema Working Group, the members of other W3C Working Groups, and industry experts in other forums who have contributed directly or indirectly to the process or content of creating this document. The Working Group is particularly grateful to Lotus Development Corp. and IBM for providing teleconferencing facilities. At the time the first edition of this specification was published, the members of the XML Schema Working Group were:

DATATYPES

Introduction

Purpose

The [XML 1.0 (Second Edition)] specification defines limited facilities for applying datatypes to document content in that documents may contain or refer to DTDs that assign types to elements and attributes. However, document authors, including authors of traditional documents and those transporting data in XML, often require a higher degree of type checking to ensure robustness in document understanding and data interchange.

The table below offers two typical examples of XML instances in which datatypes are implicit: the instance on the left represents a billing invoice, the instance on the right a memo or perhaps an e-mail message in XML.

In both cases, validity constraints exist on the content of the instances that are not expressible in XML DTDs. The limited datatyping facilities in XML have prevented validating XML processors from supplying the rigorous type checking required in these situations. The result has been that individual applications writers have had to implement type checking in an ad hoc manner. This specification addresses the need of both document authors and applications writers for a robust, extensible datatype system for XML which could be incorporated into XML processors. As discussed below, these datatypes could be used in other XML-related standards as well.

Requirements

The [XML Schema Requirements] document spells out concrete requirements to be fulfilled by this specification, which state that the XML Schema Language must: Provide for primitive data typing, including byte, date, integer, sequence, SQL and Java primitive datatypes, etc.; define a type system that is adequate for import/export from database systems (*e.g.*, relational, object, OLAP); distinguish requirements relating to lexical data representation vs. those governing an underlying information set; allow creation of user-defined datatypes, such as datatypes that are derived from existing datatypes and which may constrain certain of its properties (*e.g.*, range, precision, length, format).

1.3 Scope This portion of the XML Schema Language discusses datatypes that can be used in an XML Schema. These datatypes can be specified for element content that would be specified as #PCDATA and attribute values of various types in a DTD. It is the intention of this specification that it be usable outside of the context of XML Schemas for a wide range of other XML-related activities such as [XSL] and [RDF Schema].

Terminology

The terminology used to describe XML Schema Datatypes is defined in the body of this specification. The terms defined in the following list are used in building those definitions and in describing the actions of a datatype processor:

Definition: for compatibility A feature of this specification included solely to ensure that schemas which use this feature remain compatible with [XML 1.0 (Second Edition)]

[*Definition*:] may Conforming documents and processors are permitted to but need not behave as described.

[Definition:] match (Of strings or names:) Two strings or names being compared must be identical. Characters with multiple possible representations in ISO/IEC 10646 (*e.g.* characters with both precomposed and base+diacritic forms) match only if they have the same representation in both strings. No case folding is performed. (Of strings and rules in the grammar:) A string matches a grammatical production if it belongs to the language generated by that production.

Definition: must Conforming documents and processors are required to behave as described; otherwise they are in error.

Definition: error A violation of the rules of this specification; results are undefined. Conforming software may detect and report an error and may recover from it.

Constraints and Contributions

This specification provides three different kinds of normative statements about schema components, their representations in XML and their contribution to the schema-validation of information items:

Definition: Constraint on Schemas Constraints on the schema components themselves, *i.e.* conditions components must satisfy to be components at all. Largely to be found in Datatype components (§4).

Definition: Schema Representation Constraint Constraints on the representation of schema components in XML. Some but not all of these are expressed in Schema for Datatype Definitions (normative) (§A) and DTD for Datatype Definitions (non-normative) (§B).

Definition: Validation Rule Constraints expressed by schema components which information items must satisfy to be schema-valid. Largely to be found in Datatype components (§4).

Type System

This section describes the conceptual framework behind

the type system defined in this specification. The framework has been influenced by the [ISO 11404] standard on language-independent datatypes as well as the datatypes for [SQL] and for programming languages such as Java.

The datatypes discussed in this specification are computer representations of well known abstract concepts such as integer and date. It is not the place of this specification to define these abstract concepts; many other publications provide excellent definitions.

Datatype

Definition: In this specification, a datatype is a 3-tuple, consisting of,

1. A set of distinct values, called its value space,
2. A set of lexical representations, called its lexical space,
3. A set of facets that characterize properties of the value space, individual values or lexical items.

Value Space

Definition: A value space is the set of values for a given datatype. Each value in the value space of a datatype is denoted by one or more literals in its lexical space.

The value space of a given datatype can be defined in one of the following ways:

Defined axiomatically from fundamental notions (intensional definition) [see primitive] enumerated outright (extensional definition) [see enumeration]defined by restricting the value space of an already defined datatype to a particular subset with a given set of properties [see derived] defined as a combination of values from one or more already defined value space(s) by a specific construction procedure [see list and union] value spaces have certain properties. For example, they always have the property of cardinality, some definition of equality and might be ordered, by which individual values within the value space can be compared to one another. The properties of value spaces that are recognized by this specification are defined in Fundamental facets (§2.4.1).

Lexical Space

In addition to its value space, each datatype also has a lexical space. [Definition:] A lexical space is the set of valid literals for a datatype.

For example,"100" and"1.0E2" are two different literals from the lexical space of float which both denote the same value. The type system defined in this specification provides a mechanism for schema designers to control the set of values and the corresponding set of acceptable literals of those values for a datatype.

Note: The literals in the lexical spaces defined in this specification have the following characteristics:

- *Interoperability*: The number of literals for each value has been kept small; for many datatypes there is a one-to-one mapping between literals and values. This makes it easy to exchange the values between different systems. In many cases, conversion from locale-dependent representations will be required on both the originator and the recipient side, both for computer processing and for interaction with humans.
- *Basic readability*: Textual, rather than binary, literals are used. This makes hand editing, debugging, and similar activities possible.
- *Ease of parsing and serializing*: Where possible, literals correspond to those found in common programming languages and libraries.

Canonical Lexical Representation

While the datatypes defined in this specification have, for the most part, a single lexical representation *i.e.* each value in the datatype's value space is denoted by a single literal in its lexical space, this is not always the case.

The example in the previous section showed two literals for the datatype float which denote the same value. Similarly, there may be several literals for one of the date or time datatypes that denote the same value using different timezone indicators.

Definition: A canonical lexical representation is a set of literals from among the valid set of literals for a datatype such that there is a one-to-one mapping between literals in the canonical lexical representation and values in the value space.

Facets

Definition: A facet is a single defining aspect of a value space. Generally speaking, each facet characterizes a value space along independent axes or dimensions.

The facets of a datatype serve to distinguish those aspects of one datatype which differ from other datatypes. Rather than being defined solely in terms of a prose description the datatypes in this specification are defined in terms of the synthesis of facet values which together determine the value space and properties of the datatype.

Facets are of two types: fundamental facets that define the datatype and non-fundamental or constraining facets that constrain the permitted values of a datatype.

Fundamental facets

[Definition:] A fundamental facet is an abstract property which serves to semantically characterize the values in a value space. All fundamental facets are fully described in Fundamental Facets (4.2).

Constraining or Non-fundamental facets

Definition: A constraining facet is an optional property that can be applied to a datatype to constrain its value space.

Constraining the value space consequently constrains the lexical space. Adding constraining facets to a base type is described in Derivation by restriction (4.1.2.1).

All constraining facets are fully described in Constraining Facets (4.3).

Datatype Dichotomies

It is useful to categorize the datatypes defined in this specification along various dimensions, forming a set of characterization dichotomies.

Atomic vs. list vs. Union datatypes

The first distinction to be made is that between atomic, list and union datatypes.

Definition: Atomic datatypes are those having values which are regarded by this specification as being indivisible.

Definition: List datatypes are those having values each of which consists of a finite-length (possibly empty) sequence of values of an atomic datatype.

Definition: Union datatypes are those whose value spaces and lexical spaces are the union of the value spaces and lexical spaces of one or more other datatypes.

For example, a single token which matches Nmtoken from [XML 1.0 (Second Edition)] could be the value of an atomic datatype (NMTOKEN); while a sequence of such tokens could be the value of a list datatype (NMTOKENS).

Atomic Datatypes

atomic datatypes can be either primitive or derived. The value space of an atomic datatype is a set of"atomic" values, which for the purposes of this specification, are not further decomposable. The lexical space of an atomic datatype is a set of literals whose internal structure is specific to the datatype in question.

List Datatypes

Several type systems (such as the one described in [ISO 11404]) treat list datatypes as special cases of the more general notions of aggregate or collection datatypes. List datatypes are always derived. The value space of a list datatype is a set of finite-length sequences of atomic values. The lexical space of a list datatype is a set of literals whose internal structure is a space-separated sequence of literals of the atomic datatype of the items in the list. [Definition:] The atomic or union datatype that participates in the definition of a list datatype is known as the itemType of that list datatype.

Example:

```
<simpleType name='sizes'>
<list itemType='decimal'/>
```

```
</simpleType>
<cerealSizes xsi:type='sizes'> 8 10.5 12 </
cerealSizes>
```

A list datatype can be derived from an atomic datatype whose lexical space allows space (such as string or anyURI)or a union datatype any of whose {member type definitions}'s lexical space allows space. In such a case, regardless of the input, list items will be separated at space boundaries.

Example:

```
<simpleType name='listOfString'>
 <list itemType='string'/>
 </simpleType>
<someElement xsi:type='listOfString'>
this is not list item 1
this is not list item 2
this is not list item 3
</someElement>
```

In the above example, the value of the someElement element is not a list of length 3; rather, it is a list of length 18.

When a datatype is derived from a list datatype, the following constraining facets apply:

- Length
- MaxLength
- MinLength
- Enumeration
- Pattern
- WhiteSpace

For each of length, maxLength and minLength, the unit of length is measured in number of list items. The value of whiteSpace is fixed to the value collapse.

For list datatypes the lexical space is composed of space-separated literals of its itemType. Hence, any pattern specified when a new datatype is derived from a list datatype is matched against each literal of the list datatype and not against the literals of the datatype that serves as its itemType.

Example:

```
<xs:simpleType name='myList'>
 <xs:list itemType='xs:integer'/>
```

```
</xs:simpleType>
<xs:simpleType name='myRestrictedList'>
  <xs:restriction base='myList'>
   <xs:pattern value='123 (\d+\s)*456'/>
  </xs:restriction>
</xs:simpleType>
<someElement xsi:type='myRestrictedList'>123 456</
someElement>
<someElement xsi:type='myRestrictedList'>123 987
456</someElement>
<someElement xsi:type='myRestrictedList'>123 987
567 456</someElement>
```

The canonical-lexical-representation for the list datatype is defined as the lexical form in which each item in the list has the canonical lexical representation of its itemType.

Union Datatypes

The value space and lexical space of a union datatype are the union of the value spaces and lexical spaces of its member Types. union datatypes are always derived. Currently, there are no built-in union datatypes.

Example:

A prototypical example of a union type is the maxOccurs attribute on the element element in XML Schema itself: it is a union of nonNegativeInteger and an enumeration with the single member, the string"unbounded", as shown below.

```
<attributeGroup name="occurs">
  <attribute name="minOccurs" type=" non Negative
  Integer"
      use="optional" default="1"/>
  <attribute name="maxOccurs"use="optional"
default="1">
    <simpleType>
     <union>
      <simpleType>
       <restriction base='nonNegativeInteger'/>
      </simpleType>
      <simpleType>
```

```
        <restriction base='string'>
         <enumeration value='unbounded'/>
        </restriction>
       </simpleType>
      </union>
     </simpleType>
    </attribute>
</attributeGroup>
```

Any number (greater than 1) of atomic or list datatypes can participate in a union type.

Definition: The datatypes that participate in the definition of a union datatype are known as the memberTypes of that union datatype.

The order in which the memberTypes are specified in the definition (that is, the order of the <simpleType> children of the <union> element, or the order of the QNames in the memberTypes attribute) is significant. During validation, an element or attribute's value is validated against the memberTypes in the order in which they appear in the definition until a match is found. The evaluation order can be overridden with the use of xsi:type.

Example:

For example, given the definition below, the first instance of the <size> element validates correctly as an integer (§3.3.13), the second and third as string (§3.2.1).

```
<xsd:element name='size'>
  <xsd:simpleType>
    <xsd:union>
     <xsd:simpleType>
      <xsd:restriction base='integer'/>
     </xsd:simpleType>
     <xsd:simpleType>
     <xsd:restriction base='string'/>
    </xsd:simpleType>
   </xsd:union>
  </xsd:simpleType>
</xsd:element>
<size>1</size>
```

```
<size>large</size>
<size xsi:type='xsd:string'>1</size>
```

The canonical-lexical-representation for a union datatype is defined as the lexical form in which the values have the canonical lexical representation of the appropriate memberTypes.

Note: A datatype which is atomic in this specification need not be an"atomic" datatype in any programming language used to implement this specification. Likewise, a datatype which is a list in this specification need not be a"list" datatype in any programming language used to implement this specification. Furthermore, a datatype which is a union in this specification need not be a"union" datatype in any programming language used to implement this specification.

Primitive vs. Derived Datatypes

Next, we distinguish between primitive and derived datatypes.

Definition: Primitive datatypes are those that are not defined in terms of other datatypes; they exist ab initio.

Definition: Derived datatypes are those that are defined in terms of other datatypes.

For example, in this specification, float is a well-defined mathematical concept that cannot be defined in terms of other datatypes, while a integer is a special case of the more general datatype decimal.

Definition: The simple ur-type definition is a special restriction of the ur-type definition whose name is anySimpleType in the XML Schema namespace. anySimpleType can be considered as the base type of all primitive datatypes. anySimpleType is considered to have an unconstrained lexical space and a value space consisting of the union of the value spaces of all the primitive datatypes and the set of all lists of all members of the value spaces of all the primitive datatypes.

The datatypes defined by this specification fall into both the primitive and derived categories. It is felt that a judiciously chosen set of primitive datatypes will serve the widest possible audience by providing a set of convenient datatypes that can be used as is, as well as providing a rich enough base from which the variety of datatypes needed by schema designers can be derived. In the example above, integer is derived from decimal.

Note: A datatype which is primitive in this specification need not be a"primitive" datatype in any programming language used to implement this specification. Likewise, a datatype which is derived in this specification need not be a"derived" datatype in any programming language used to implement this specification.

As described in more detail in XML Representation of Simple Type Definition Schema Components (§4.1.2), each user-derived datatype must be defined in terms of another datatype in one of three ways:

1. By assigning constraining facets which serve to restrict the value space of the user-derived datatype to a subset of that of the base type;
2. By creating a list datatype whose value space consists of finite-length sequences of values of its itemType;
3. By creating a union datatype whose value space consists of the union of the value spaces of its memberTypes.

Derived by Restriction

- *Definition*: A datatype is said to be derived by restriction from another datatype when values for zero or more constraining facets are specified that serve to constrain its value space and/or its lexical space to a subset of those of its base type.
- *Definition*: Every datatype that is derived by restriction is defined in terms of an existing datatype, referred to as its base type. base types can be either primitive or derived.
- *Derived by list*: A list datatype can be derived from another datatype (its itemType) by creating a value space that consists of a finite-length sequence of values of its itemType.

- *Derived by union*: One datatype can be derived from one or more datatypes by unioning their value spaces and, consequently, their lexical spaces.

Built-in vs. User-derived Datatypes

Definition: Built-in datatypes are those which are defined in this specification, and can be either primitive or derived;

Definition: User-derived datatypes are those derived datatypes that are defined by individual schema designers.

Conceptually there is no difference between the built-in derived datatypes included in this specification and the user-derived datatypes which will be created by individual schema designers. The built-in derived datatypes are those which are believed to be so common that if they were not defined in this specification many schema designers would end up"reinventing" them. Furthermore, including these derived datatypes in this specification serves to demonstrate the mechanics and utility of the datatype generation facilities of this specification.

Note: A datatype which is built-in in this specification need not be a"built-in" datatype in any programming language used to implement this specification. Likewise, a datatype which is user-derived in this specification need not be a"user-derived" datatype in any programming language used to implement this specification.

Built-in datatypes: Each built-in datatype in this specification (both primitive and derived) can be uniquely addressed via a URI Reference constructed as follows:

- The base URI is the URI of the XML Schema namespace
- The fragment identifier is the name of the datatype
- For example, to address the int datatype, the URI is:
- Additionally, each facet definition element can be uniquely addressed via a URI constructed as follows:
- The base URI is the URI of the XML Schema namespace
- The fragment identifier is the name of the facet

For example, to address the maxInclusive facet, the URI is:

Additionally, each facet usage in a built-in datatype definition can be uniquely addressed via a URI constructed as follows:

- The base URI is the URI of the XML Schema namespace
- The fragment identifier is the name of the datatype, followed by a period (".") followed by the name of the facet
- *For example, to address the usage of the maxInclusive facet in the definition of int, the URI is:*

Namespace Considerations

The built-in datatypes defined by this specification are designed to be used with the XML Schema definition language as well as other XML specifications. To facilitate usage within the XML Schema definition language, the built-in datatypes in this specification have the namespace name:

To facilitate usage in specifications other than the XML Schema definition language, such as those that do not want to know anything about aspects of the XML Schema definition language other than the datatypes, each built-in datatype is also defined in the namespace whose URI is:

This applies to both built-in primitive and built-in derived datatypes. Each user-derived datatype is also associated with a unique namespace. However, user-derived datatypes do not come from the namespace defined by this specification; rather, they come from the namespace of the schema in which they are defined.

Primitive Datatypes

The primitive datatypes defined by this specification are described below. For each datatype, the value space and lexical space are defined, constraining facets which apply to the datatype are listed and any datatypes derived from this datatype are specified. Primitive datatypes can only be added by revisions to this specification.

String

Definition: The string datatype represents character strings in XML. The value space of string is the set of finite-length sequences of characters (as defined in [XML 1.0 (Second Edition)]) that match the Char production from [XML 1.0 (Second Edition)]. A character is an atomic unit of communication; it is not further specified except to note that every character has a corresponding Universal Character Set code point, which is an integer.

Note: Many human languages have writing systems that require child elements for control of aspects such as bidirectional formating or ruby annotation (see [Ruby] and Section 8.2.4 Overriding the bidirectional algorithm: the BDO element of [HTML 4.01]).

Thus, string, as a simple type that can contain only characters but not child elements, is often not suitable for representing text. In such situations, a complex type that allows mixed content should be considered. For more information, see Section 5.5 Any Element, Any Attribute of [XML Schema Language: Part 0 Primer].

Note: As noted in ordered, the fact that this specification does not specify an order-relation for string does not preclude other applications from treating strings as being ordered.

Constraining Facets

String has the following constraining Facets:

- Length
- MinLength
- MaxLength
- Pattern
- Enumeration
- WhiteSpace

Derived Datatypes

The following built-in datatypes are derived from string: normalizedString

Boolean

Definition: boolean has the value space required to support the mathematical concept of binary-valued logic: {true, false}.

Lexical Representation

An instance of a datatype that is defined as boolean can have the following legal literals {true, false, 1, 0}.

Canonical Representation

The canonical representation for boolean is the set of literals {true, false}.

Constraining Facets

Boolean has the following constraining facets:

- Pattern
- WhiteSpace

Decimal

Definition: decimal represents a subset of the real numbers, which can be represented by decimal numerals. The

Main Features

- XML syntax (there is a Schema for Schemas)
- Uses and supports Namespaces
- Object-oriented-like type system for declarations (with inheritance, subsumption, abstract types, and finals)
- Global (=top-level) and local (=inlined) type definitions
- Modularization (schema inclusion and redefinitions)
- Structured self-documentation
- Cardinality constraints for sub-elements
- Nil values (missing content)
- Attribute and element defaults
- Any-element, any-attribute
- Uniqueness constraints and ID/IDREF attribute scope
- Regular expressions for specifying valid chardata and attribute values
- Lots of built-in data types for chardata and attribute values

6

CSS

INTRODUCTION

CSS stands for Cascading Style Sheets. It is a way to divide the content from the layout on web pages.

HOW IT WORKS

- A style is a definition of fonts, colours, etc.
- Each style has a unique name: a selector.
- The selectors and their styles are defined in one place.

In your HTML contents you simply refer to the selectors whenever you want to activate a certain style.

HOW DOES CSS WORK

In this lesson you will learn how to make your first style sheet. You will get to know about the basic CSS model and which codes are necessary to use CSS in an HTML document.

Many of the properties used in Cascading Style Sheets (CSS) are similar to those of HTML. Thus, if you are used to use HTML for layout, you will most likely recognize many of the codes. Let us look at a concrete example.

The Basic CSS Syntax

Let's say we want a nice red colour as the background of a webpage:

Using HTML we could have done it like this:

```
<body bgcolour="#FF0000">
```

With CSS the same result can be achieved like this:

```
body {background-colour: #FF0000;}
```

Applying CSS to an HTML Document

There are three ways you can apply CSS to an HTML document. These methods are all outlined below. We recommend that you focus on the third method *i.e.* external.

Method 1: In-line (the Attribute Style)

One way to apply CSS to HTML is by using the HTML attribute style. Building on the above example with the red background colour, it can be applied like this:

```
<html>
  <head>
   <title>Example</title>
  </head>
  <body style="background-colour: #FF0000;">
   <p>This is a red page</p>
  </body>
</html>
```

Method 2: Internal (the Tag Style)

Another way is to include the CSS codes using the HTML tag <style>.

For example like this:

```
<html>
  <head>
   <title>Example</title>
   <style type="text/css">
    body {background-colour: #FF0000;}
   </style>
  </head>
  <body>
   <p>This is a red page</p>
  </body>
</html>
```

Method 3: External (Link to a Style Sheet)

The recommended method is to link to a so-called external style sheet. Throughout this tutorial we will use this method in all our examples.

An external style sheet is simply a text file with the extension.css. Like any other file, you can place the style sheet on your web server or hard disk.

For example, let's say that your style sheet is named style.css and is located in a folder named style. The situation can be illustrated like this:

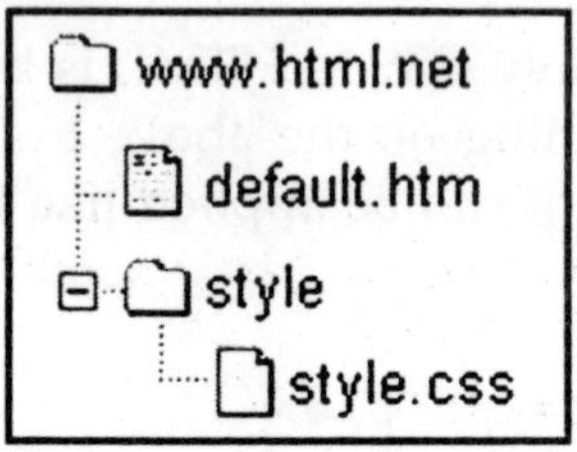

The trick is to create a link from the HTML document (default.htm) to the style sheet (style.css). Such link can be created with one line of HTML code:

```
<link rel="stylesheet" type="text/css"
   href="style/style.css"/>
```

Notice how the path to our style sheet is indicated using the attribute href.

The line of code must be inserted in the header section of the HTML code i.e. between the <head> and</head> tags. Like this:

```
<html>
  <head>
   <title>My document</title>
   <link rel="stylesheet" type="text/css"
     href="style/style.css"/>
  </head>
  <body>
  ...
```

This link tells the browser that it should use the layout from the CSS file when displaying the HTML file.

The really smart thing is that several HTML documents can be linked to the same style sheet. In other words, one CSS file can be used to control the layout of many HTML documents.

This technique can save you a lot of work. If you, for example, would like to change the background colour of a website with 100 pages, a style sheet can save you from having to manually change all 100 HTML documents. Using CSS, the change can be made in a few seconds just by changing one code in the central style sheet. Let's put what we just learned into practice.

What is the Difference Between CSS and HTML

HTML is used to structure content. CSS is used for formatting structured content. Okay, it sounds a bit technical and confusing. But please continue reading. It will all make sense to you soon. Back in the good old days when Madonna was a virgin and a guy called Tim Berners Lee invented the World Wide Web, the language HTML was only used to add structure to text. An author could mark his text by stating"this is a headline" or"this is a paragraph" using HTML tags such as <h1> and <p>.

As the Web gained popularity, designers started looking for possibilities to add layout to online documents. To meet this demand, the browser producers (at that time Netscape and Microsoft) invented new HTML tags such as for example <font> which differed from the original HTML tags by defining layout–and not structure. This also led to a situation where original structure tags such as <table> were increasingly being misused to layout pages instead of adding structure to text. Many new layout tags such as <blink> were only supported by one type of browser."You need browser X to view this page" became a common disclaimer on web sites.

CSS was invented to remedy this situation by providing web designers with sophisticated layout opportunities supported by all browsers. At the same time, separation of the presentation style of documents from the content of documents, makes site maintenance a lot easier.

Which Benefits will CSS give me

CSS was a revolution in the world of web design. The concrete benefits of CSS include:

- Control layout of many documents from one single style sheet;

- More precise control of layout;
- Apply different layout to different media-types (screen, print, etc.);
- Numerous advanced and sophisticated techniques.

ADVANTAGES

With CSS, you will be able to:

- Define the look of your pages in one place rather than repeating yourself over and over again throughout your site. (Ever get tired of defining colours and fonts each time you start a new cell in a table? Those days are over with CSS!)
- Easily change the look of your pages even after they're created. Since the styles are defined in one place you can change the look of the entire site at once. (Ever get tired of replacing tags throughout your site when you want to change the look of a certain element? Those days are over with CSS!)
- Define font sizes and similar attributes with the same accuracy as you have with a word processor–not being limited to just the seven different font sizes defined in HTML.
- Position the content of your pages with pixel precision.
- Redefine entire HTML tags. Say for example, if you wanted the bold tag to be red using a special font–this can be done easily with CSS.
- Define customised styles for links–such as getting rid of the underline.
- Define layers that can be positioned on top of each other (often used for menus that pop up).

STARTING WITH HTML + CSS

This short tutorial is meant for people who want to start using CSS and have never written a CSS style sheet before.

It does not explain much of CSS. It just explains how to create an HTML file, a CSS file and how to make them work together. After that, you can read any of a number of other tutorials to add more features to the HTML and CSS files. Or you can switch to using a dedicated HTML or CSS editor, that helps you set up complex sites.

At the end of the tutorial, you will have made an HTML file that looks like this: The resulting HTML page, with colours and layout, all done with CSS.

Note that I don't claim that this is beautiful

Sections that look like this are optional. They contain some extra explanation of the HTML and CSS codes in the example. The"alert!" sign at the start indicates that this is more advanced material than the rest of the text.

WRITING THE HTML

For this tutorial, I suggest you use only the very simplest of tools. *E.g.*, Notepad (under Windows), TextEdit (on the Mac) or KEdit (under KDE) will do fine. Once you understand the principles, you may want to switch to more advanced tools, or even to commercial programmes, such as Style Master, Dreamweaver or GoLive. But for your very first CSS style sheet, it is good not to be distracted by too many advanced features.

Don't use a wordprocessor, such as Microsoft Word or OpenOffice. They typically make files that a Web browser cannot read. For HTML and CSS, we want simple, plain text files.

Step 1 is to open your text editor (Notepad, TextEdit, KEdit, or whatever is your favourite), start with an empty window and type the following:

```
<!DOCTYPE html PUBLIC"-//W3C//DTD HTML 4.01//
EN">
<html>
<head>
 <title>My first styled page</title>
</head>
<body>
<!-- Site navigation menu -->
<ul class="navbar">
 <li><a href="index.html">Home page</a>
```

```
 <li><a href="musings.html">Musings</a>
 <li><a href="town.html">My town</a>
 <li><a href="links.html">Links</a>
</ul>
<!-- Main content -->
<h1>My first styled page</h1>
<p>Welcome to my styled page!
<p>It lacks images, but at least it has style.
   And it has links, even if they don't go
   anywhereandhellip;
<p>There should be more here, but I don't know
what yet.
<!-- Sign and date the page, it's only polite!
-->
<address>Made 5 April 2004<br>
by myself.</address>
</body>
</html>
```

In fact, you don't have to type it: you can copy and paste it from this Web page into the editor.

(If you are using TextEdit on the Mac, don't forget to tell TextEdit that the text is really plain text, by going to the Format menu and selecting"Make plain text".)

The first line of the HTML file above tells the browser which type of HTML this is (DOCTYPE means DOCument TYPE). In this case, it is HTML version 4.01.

Words within < and > are called tags and, as you can see, the document is contained within the <html> and </html> tags. Between <head> and </head> there is room for various kinds of information that is not shown on screen. So far it contains the title of the document, but later we will add the CSS style sheet there, too.

The <body> is where the actual text of the document goes. In principle, everything in there will be displayed, except for the the text inside <!-- and -->, which serves as a comment to ourselves. The browser will ignore it.

Of the tags in the example, <ul> introduces an"Unordered List", *i.e.*, a list in which the items are not numbered. The <li>

is the start of a"List Item." The <p> is a"Paragraph." And the <a> is an"Anchor," which is what creates a hyperlink.

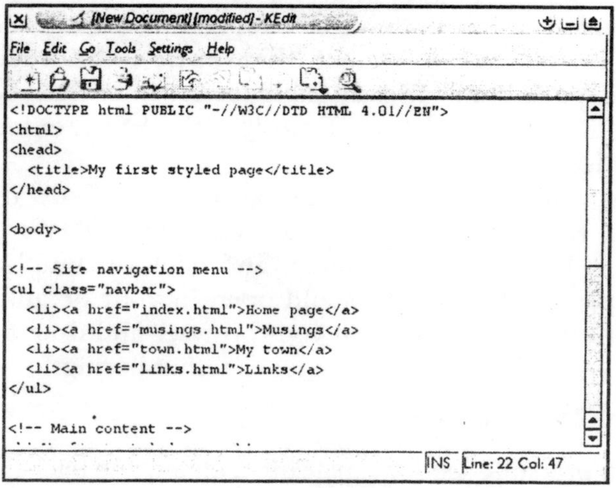

FIg. The KEdit Editor Showing the HTML Source.

If you want to know what the names in <...> mean, one good place to start is Getting started with HTML. But just a few words about the structure of our example HTML page.

The"ul" is a list with one hyperlink per item. This will serve as our"site navigation menu," linking to the other pages of our (hypothetical) Web site. Presumably, all pages on our site have a similar menu.

The"h1" and"p" elements form the unique content of this page, while the signature at the bottom ("address") will again be similar on all pages of the site.

Note that I didn't close the"li" and"p" elements. In HTML (but not in XHTML), it is allowed to omit the </li> and </p> tags, which I did here, to make the text a little easier to read. But you may add them, if you prefer.

Let's assume that this is going to be one page of a Web site with several similar pages. As is common for current Web pages, this one has a menu that links to other pages on the hypothetical site, some unique content and a signature.

Now select"Save As..." from the File menu, navigate to a directory/folder where you want to put it (the Desktop is fine) and save the file as"mypage.html". Don't close the editor yet, we will need it again.

(If you are using TextEdit on Mac OS X before version 10.4, you will see an option Don't append the.txt extension in the Save as dialog. Select that option, because the name"mypage.html" already includes an extension. Newer versions of TextEdit will notice the.html extension automatically.)

Next, open the file in a browser. You can do that as follows: find the file with your file manager (Windows Explorer, Finder or Konqueror) and click or double click the"mypage.html" file. It should open in your default Web browser. (If it does not, open your browser and drag the file to it.) As you can see, the page looks rather boring...

ADDING SOME COLOURS

You probably see some black text on a white background, but it depends on how the browser is configured. So one easy thing we can do to make the page more stylish is to add some colours. (Leave the browser open, we will use it again later.)

We will start with a style sheet embedded inside the HTML file. Later, we will put the HTML and the CSS in separate files. Separate files is good, since it makes it easier to use the same style sheet for multiple HTML files: you only have to write the style sheet once. But for this step, we just keep everything in one file.

We need to add a <style> element to the HTML file. The style sheet will be inside that element. So go back to the editor window and add the following five lines in the head part of the HTML file. The lines to add are shown in red.

```
<!DOCTYPE html PUBLIC"-//W3C//DTD HTML 4.01//
EN">
<html>
<head>
  <title>My first styled page</title>
  <style type="text/css">
body {
  colour: purple;
```

```
  background-colour: #d8da3d}
  </style>
</head>
<body>
[etc.]
```

The first line says that this is a style sheet and that it is written in CSS ("text/css"). The second line says that we add style to the"body" element. The third line sets the colour of the text to purple and the next line sets the background to a sort of greenish yellow.

Style sheets in CSS are made up of rules. Each rule has three parts:

- The selector (in the example:"body"), which tells the browser which part of the document is affected by the rule;
- The property (in the example,'colour' and'background-colour' are both properties), which specifies what aspect of the layout is being set;
- The value ('purple' and'#d8da3d'), which gives the value for the style property.

The example shows that rules can be combined. We have set two properties, so we could have made two separate rules:

```
body {colour: purple}
body {background-colour: #d8da3d}
```

but since both rules affect the body, we only wrote"body" once and put the properties and values together. For more about selectors.

The background of the body element will also be the background of the whole document. We haven't given any of the other elements (p, li, address...) any explicit background, so by default they will have none (or: will be transparent). The'colour' property sets the colour of the text for the body element, but all other elements inside the body inherit that colour, unless explicitly overridden.

ADDING FONTS

Another thing that is easy to do is to make some distinction in the fonts for the various elements of the page.

So let's set the text in the"Georgia" font, except for the h1 heading, which we'll give"Helvetica."

On the Web, you can never be sure what fonts your readers have on their computers, so we add some alternatives as well: if Georgia is not available, Times New Roman or Times are also fine, and if all else fails, the browser may use any other font with serifs.

If Helvetica is absent, Geneva, Arial and SunSans-Regular are quite similar in shape, and if none of these work, the browser can choose any other font that is serif-less.

In the text editor add the following lines:

```
<!DOCTYPE html PUBLIC"-//W3C//DTD HTML 4.01//
EN">
<html>
<head>
 <title>My first styled page</title>
 <style type="text/css">
 body {
  font-family: Georgia,"Times New Roman",
   Times, serif;
 colour: purple;
 background-colour: #d8da3d}
h1 {
 font-family: Helvetica, Geneva, Arial,
  SunSans-Regular, sans-serif}
 </style>
</head>
<body>
[etc.]
```

ADDING A NAVIGATION BAR

The list at the top of the HTML page is meant to become a navigation menu. Many Web sites have some sort of menu along the top or on the side of the page and this page should have one as well. We will put it on the left side, because that is a little more interesting than at the top...

The menu is already in the HTML page. It is the <ul> list at the top. The links in it don't work, since our"Web site" so far consists of only one page, but that doesn't matter now. On a real Web site, there should not be any broken links, of course. So we need to move the list to the left and move the rest of the text a little to the right, to make room for it. The CSS properties we use for that are'padding-left' (to move the body text) and'position','left' and'top' (to move the menu).

```
<!DOCTYPE html PUBLIC"-//W3C//DTD HTML 4.01//
EN">
<html>
<head>
  <title>My first styled page</title>
  <style type="text/css">
  body {
   padding-left: 11em;
   font-family: Georgia,"Times New Roman",
    Times, serif;
  colour: purple;
  background-colour: #d8da3d}
  ul.navbar {
  position: absolute;
  top: 2em;
  left: 1em;
  width: 9em}
h1 {
  font-family: Helvetica, Geneva, Arial,
    SunSans-Regular, sans-serif}
  </style>
</head>
<body>
[etc.]
```

STYLING THE LINKS

The navigation menu still looks like a list, instead of a menu. Let's add some style to it. We'll remove the list bullet and move the items to the left, to where the bullet was. We'll also give each item its own white background and a black square. (Why? No particular reason, just because we can.) We also haven't said what the colours of the links should be, so let's add that as well: blue for links that the user hasn't seen yet and purple for links already visited:

```
<!DOCTYPE html PUBLIC"-//W3C//DTD HTML 4.01//
EN">
<html>
<head>
  <title>My first styled page</title>
  <style type="text/css">
  body {
  padding-left: 11em;
  font-family: Georgia,"Times New Roman",
  Times, serif;
  colour: purple;
  background-colour: #d8da3d}
  ul.navbar {
   list-style-type: none;
   padding: 0;
   margin: 0;
   position: absolute;
   top: 2em;
   left: 1em;
   width: 9em}
h1 {
  font-family: Helvetica, Geneva, Arial,
   SunSans-Regular, sans-serif}
ul.navbar li {
   background: white;
   margin: 0.5em 0;
   padding: 0.3em;
   border-right: 1em solid black}
ul.navbar a {
   text-decoration: none}
a:link {
   colour: blue}
a:visited {
   colour: purple}
</style>
</head>
```

```
<body>
[etc.]
```

Traditionally, browsers show hyperlinks with underlines and with colours. Usually, the colours are similar to what we specificed here: blue for links to pages that you haven't visited yet (or visited a long time ago), purple for pages that you have already seen.

In HTML, hyperlinks are created with <a> elements, so to specify the colour, we need to add a style rule for"a". To differentiate between visited and unvisited links, CSS provides two"pseudo-classes" (:link and:visited). They are called"pseudo-classes" to distinguish them from class attributes, that appear in the HTML directly, *e.g.*, the class="navbar"in our example.

ADDING A HORIZONTAL LINE

The final addition to the style sheet is a horizontal rule to separate the text from the signature at the bottom. We will use'border-top' to add a dotted line above the <address> element:

```
<!DOCTYPE html PUBLIC"-//W3C//DTD HTML 4.01//
EN">
<html>
<head>
  <title>My first styled page</title>
  <style type="text/css">
  body {
  padding-left: 11em;
  font-family: Georgia,"Times New Roman",
   Times, serif;
  colour: purple;
  background-colour: #d8da3d}
ul.navbar {
  list-style-type: none;
  padding: 0;
  margin: 0;
  position: absolute;
  top: 2em;
```

```
  left: 1em;
  width: 9em}
h1 {
font-family: Helvetica, Geneva, Arial,
  SunSans-Regular, sans-serif}
ul.navbar li {
  background: white;
  margin: 0.5em 0;
  padding: 0.3em;
  border-right: 1em solid black}
ul.navbar a {
  text-decoration: none}
a:link {
  colour: blue}
a:visited {
  colour: purple}
address {
  margin-top: 1em;
  padding-top: 1em;
  border-top: thin dotted}
  </style>
</head>
<body>
[etc.]
```

Now our style is complete. Next, let's look at how we can put the style sheet in a separate file, so that other pages can share the same style.

PUTTING THE STYLE SHEET IN A SEPARATE FILE

We now have an HTML file with an embedded style sheet. But if our site grows we probably want many pages to share the same style. There is a better method than copying the style sheet into every page: if we put the style sheet in a separate file, all pages can point to it.

To make a style sheet file, we need to create another empty text file. You can choose"New" from the File menu in the editor, to create an empty window. (If you are using TextEdit, don't forget to make it plain text again, using the Format menu.)

Then cut and paste everything that is inside the <style> element from the HTML file into the new window. Don't copy the <style> and </style> themselves. They belong to HTML, not to CSS. In the new editor window, you should now have the complete style sheet:

```
body {
 padding-left: 11em;
 font-family: Georgia,"Times New Roman",
  Times, serif;
colour: purple;
 background-colour: #d8da3d}
ul.navbar {
 list-style-type: none;
 padding: 0;
 margin: 0;
 position: absolute;
 top: 2em;
 left: 1em;
 width: 9em}
h1 {
font-family: Helvetica, Geneva, Arial,
 SunSans-Regular, sans-serif}
ul.navbar li {
 background: white;
 margin: 0.5em 0;
 padding: 0.3em;
 border-right: 1em solid black}
ul.navbar a {
 text-decoration: none}
a:link {
 colour: blue}
a:visited {
 colour: purple}
address {
 margin-top: 1em;
 padding-top: 1em;
```

```
 border-top: thin dotted}
```

Choose"Save As..." from the File menu, make sure that you are in the same directory/folder as the mypage.html file, and save the style sheet as"mystyle.css".

Now go back to the window with the HTML code. Remove everything from the <style> tag up to and including the </style> tag and replace it with a <link> element, as follows:

```
<!DOCTYPE html PUBLIC"-//W3C//DTD HTML 4.01//
EN">
<html>
<head>
  <title>My first styled page</title>
  <link rel="stylesheet" href="mystyle.css">
</head>
<body>
[etc.]
```

This will tell the browser that the style sheet is found in the file called"mystyle.css" and since no directory is mentioned, the browser will look in the same directory where it found the HTML file. If you save the HTML file and reload it in the browser, you should see no change: the page is still styled the same way, but now the style comes from an external file.

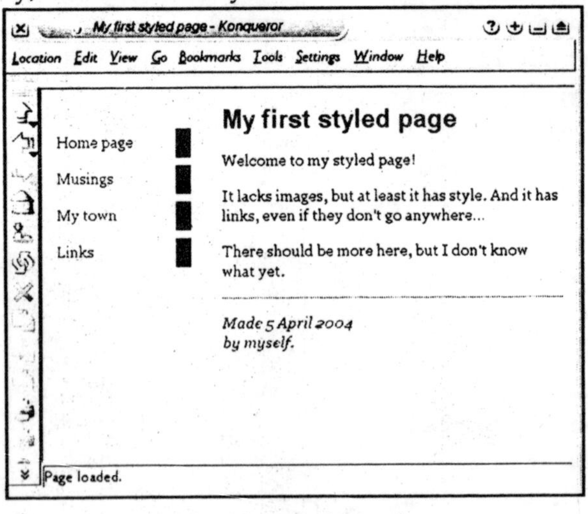

Fig. The Final Result

The next step is to put both files, mypage.html and mystyle.css on your Web site. (Well, you might want to change them a bit first…) But how to do that depends on your Internet provider.

- HTML and XML–structuring information for the future (24 pp.)
- Namespaces, XInclude, and XML Base–common extensions to the XML specification (9 pp.)
- DTD, XML Schema, and DSD–defining language syntax with schemas (28 pp.)
- XLink, XPointer, and XPath–linking and addressing (26 pp.)
- XSL and XSLT–stylesheets and document transformation (21 pp.)
- XQuery–document querying (19 pp.)
- DOM, SAX, and JDOM–programming for XML (17 pp.)
- W3C -

7

XML Debugging

ERRORS

Different kinds of errors can occur in a programme, and it is useful to distinguish among them in order to track them down more quickly.

- Syntax errors are produced by Python when it is translating the source code into byte code. They usually indicate that there is something wrong with the syntax of the programme. Example: Omitting the colon at the end of adef statement yields the somewhat redundant message SyntaxError: invalid syntax.
- Runtime errors are produced by the runtime system if something goes wrong while the programme is running. Most runtime error messages include information about where the error occurred and what functions were executing. Example: An infinite recursion eventually causes a runtime error of "maximum recursion depth exceeded."
- Semantic errors are problems with a programme that compiles and runs but doesn't do the right thing. Example: An expression may not be evaluated in the order you expect, yielding an unexpected result.

The first step in debugging is to figure out which kind of error you are dealing with.

Although the following sections are organized by error type, some techniques are applicable in more than one situation.

Syntax errors: Syntax errors are usually easy to fix once you figure out what they are. Unfortunately, the error messages are often not helpful. The most common messages are SyntaxError: invalid syntax and SyntaxError: invalid token, neither of which is very informative.

On the other hand, the message does tell you where in the programme the problem occurred. Actually, it tells you where Python noticed a problem, which is not necessarily where the error is. Sometimes the error is prior to the location of the error message, often on the preceding line.

If you are building the programme incrementally, you should have a good idea about where the error is. It will be in the last line you added.

If you are copying code from a book, start by comparing your code to the book's code very carefully. Check every character. At the same time, remember that the book might be wrong, so if you see something that looks like a syntax error, it might be.

WAYS TO AVOID COMMON SYNTAX ERRORS

- Make sure you are not using a Python keyword for a variable name.
- Check that you have a colon at the end of the header of every compound statement, including for, while, if, and def statements.
- Check that indentation is consistent. You may indent with either spaces or tabs but it's best not to mix them. Each level should be nested the same amount.
- Make sure that any strings in the code have matching quotation marks.
- If you have multiline strings with triple quotes (single or double), make sure you have terminated the string properly. An unterminated string may cause an invalid token error at the end of your programme, or it may treat the following part of the programme as a string until it comes to the next string. In the second case, it might not produce an error message at all!

- An unclosed bracket (, {, or [makes Python continue with the next line as part of the current statement. Generally, an error occurs almost immediately in the next line.
- Check for the classic = instead of == inside a conditional.

If the compiler says there is an error and you don't see it, that might be because you and the compiler are not looking at the same code. Check your programming environment to make sure that the programme you are editing is the one Python is trying to run. If you are not sure, try putting an obvious and deliberate syntax error at the beginning of the programme. Now run (or import) it again. If the compiler doesn't find the new error, there is probably something wrong with the way your environment is set up.

If this happens, one approach is to start again with a new programme like "Hello, World!," and make sure you can get a known programme to run. Then gradually add the pieces of the new programme to the working one.

RUNTIME ERRORS

Once your programme is syntactically correct, Python can import it and at least start running it. What could possibly go wrong?

MY PROGRAMME DOES ABSOLUTELY NOTHING

This problem is most common when your file consists of functions and classes but does not actually invoke anything to start execution. This may be intentional if you only plan to import this module to supply classes and functions.

If it is not intentional, make sure that you are invoking a function to start execution, or execute one from the interactive prompt. Also see the "Flow of Execution" section below.

MY PROGRAMME HANGS

If a programme stops and seems to be doing nothing, we say it is "hanging." Often that means that it is caught in an infinite loop or an infinite recursion.

- If there is a particular loop that you suspect is the problem, add a printstatement immediately before the loop that says "entering the loop" and another immediately after that says "exiting the loop."

Run the programme: If you get the first message and not the second, you've got an infinite loop. Go to the "Infinite Loop" section below.

- Most of the time, an infinite recursion will cause the programme to run for a while and then produce a "RuntimeError: Maximum recursion depth exceeded" error. If that happens, go to the "Infinite Recursion" section below.

If you are not getting this error but you suspect there is a problem with a recursive method or function, you can still use the techniques in the "Infinite Recursion" section.

- If neither of those steps works, start testing other loops and other recursive functions and methods.
- If that doesn't work, then it is possible that you don't understand the flow of execution in your programme. Go to the "Flow of Execution" section below.

INFINITE LOOP

If you think you have an infinite loop and you think you know what loop is causing the problem, add a print statement at the end of the loop that prints the values of the variables in the condition and the value of the condition.

For example:

```
while x > 0 and y < 0:
    # do something to x
    # do something to y
print "x: ", x
print "y: ", y
print "condition: ", (x > 0 and y < 0)
```

Now when you run the programme, you will see three lines of output for each time through the loop. The last time through the loop, the condition should be false. If the loop keeps going, you will be able to see the values of x and y, and you might figure out why they are not being updated correctly.

INFINITE RECURSION

Most of the time, an infinite recursion will cause the programme to run for a while and then produce a Maximum recursion depth exceeded error. If you suspect that a function or method is causing an infinite recursion, start by checking to make sure that there is a base case. In other words, there should be some condition that will cause the function or method to return without making a recursive invocation. If not, then you need to rethink the algorithm and identify a base case.

If there is a base case but the programme doesn't seem to be reaching it, add a print statement at the beginning of the function or method that prints the parameters. Now when you run the programme, you will see a few lines of output every time the function or method is invoked, and you will see the parameters. If the parameters are not moving towards the base case, you will get some ideas about why not.

FLOW OF EXECUTION

If you are not sure how the flow of execution is moving through your programme, add print statements to the beginning of each function with a message like "entering function foo," where foo is the name of the function.

Now when you run the programme, it will print a trace of each function as it is invoked.

EXCEPTION ON RUNNING PROGRAMME

If something goes wrong during runtime, Python prints a message that includes the name of the exception, the line of the programme where the problem occurred, and a traceback.

The traceback identifies the function that is currently running, and then the function that invoked it, and then the function that invoked *that*, and so on. In other words, it traces the path of function invocations that got you to where you are. It also includes the line number in your file where each of these calls occurs. The first step is to examine the place in the programme where the error occurred and see if you can figure out what happened. These are some of the most common runtime errors:

Name Error

You are trying to use a variable that doesn't exist in the current environment. Remember that local variables are local. You cannot refer to them from outside the function where they are defined.

Type Error

There are several possible causes:

- You are trying to use a value improperly. *Example*: indexing a string, list, or tuple with something other than an integer.
- There is a mismatch between the items in a format string and the items passed for conversion. This can happen if either the number of items does not match or an invalid conversion is called for.
- You are passing the wrong number of arguments to a function or method. For methods, look at the method definition and check that the first parameter is self. Then look at the method invocation; make sure you are invoking the method on an object with the right type and providing the other arguments correctly.

Key Error

You are trying to access an element of a dictionary using a key value that the dictionary does not contain.

Attribute Error

You are trying to access an attribute or method that does not exist.

Index Error

The index you are using to access a list, string, or tuple is greater than its length minus one. Immediately before the site of the error, add a printstatement to display the value of the index and the length of the array. Is the array the right size? Is the index the right value?

I added so many print statements I get inundated with output. One of the problems with using print statements for debugging is that you can end up buried in output. There are two ways to proceed: simplify the output or simplify the programme. To simplify the output, you can remove or comment out print statements that aren't helping, or combine them, or format the output so it is easier to understand.

To simplify the programme, there are several things you can do. First, scale down the problem the programme is working on. For example, if you are sorting an array, sort a *small* array. If the programme takes input from the user, give it the simplest input that causes the problem.

Second, clean up the programme. Remove dead code and reorganize the programme to make it as easy to read as possible. For example, if you suspect that the problem is in a deeply nested part of the programme, try rewriting that part with simpler structure. If you suspect a large function, try splitting it into smaller functions and testing them separately.

Often the process of finding the minimal test case leads you to the bug. If you find that a programme works in one situation but not in another, that gives you a clue about what is going on. Similarly, rewriting a piece of code can help you find subtle bugs. If you make a change that you think doesn't affect the programme, and it does, that can tip you off.

Semantic Errors

In some ways, semantic errors are the hardest to debug, because the compiler and the runtime system provide no information about what is wrong. Only you know what the programme is supposed to do, and only you know that it isn't doing it.

The first step is to make a connection between the programme text and the behaviour you are seeing. You need a hypothesis about what the programme is actually doing. One of the things that makes that hard is that computers run so fast.

You will often wish that you could slow the programme down to human speed, and with some debuggers you can. But the time it takes to insert a few well-placedprint statements is often short compared to setting up the debugger, inserting and removing breakpoints, and "walking" the programme to where the error is occurring.

PROGRAMME DOESN'T WORK

You should ask yourself these questions:

- Is there something the programme was supposed to do but which doesn't seem to be happening? Find the section of the code that performs that function and make sure it is executing when you think it should.
- *Is something happening that shouldn't*: Find code in your programme that performs that function and see if it is executing when it shouldn't.
- *Is a section of code producing an effect that is not what you expected*: Make sure that you understand the code in question, especially if it involves invocations to functions or methods in other Python modules. Read the documentation for the functions you invoke. Try them out by writing simple test cases and checking the results.

In order to programme, you need to have a mental model of how programmes work. If you write a programme that doesn't do what you expect, very often the problem is not in the programme; it's in your mental model.

The best way to correct your mental model is to break the programme into its components (usually the functions and methods) and test each component independently. Once you find the discrepancy between your model and reality, you can solve the problem.

Of course, you should be building and testing components as you develop the programme. If you encounter a problem, there should be only a small amount of new code that is not known to be correct.

Beyong Expectation

Writing complex expressions is fine as long as they are

readable, but they can be hard to debug. It is often a good idea to break a complex expression into a series of assignments to temporary variables.

For example:

```
self.hands[i].addCard (self.hands [self. find
Neighbour (i)]. popCard())
```

This can be rewritten as:

```
neighbour = self.findNeighbour (i)
pickedCard = self.hands[neighbour].popCard()
self.hands[i].addCard (pickedCard)
```

The explicit version is easier to read because the variable names provide additional documentation, and it is easier to debug because you can check the types of the intermediate variables and display their values.

Whenever you are not sure of the order of evaluation, use parentheses. Not only will the programme be correct (in the sense of doing what you intended), it will also be more readable for other people who haven't memorized the rules of precedence.

I've got a function or method that doesn't return what I expect. If you have a **return** statement with a complex expression, you don't have a chance to print the **return** value before returning. Again, you can use a temporary variable.

For example, instead of:

```
return self.hands[i].removeMatches()
```

you could write:

```
count = self.hands[i].removeMatches()
return count
```

Now you have the opportunity to display the value of count before returning.

I'm really, really stuck and I need help. First, try getting away from the computer for a few minutes. Computers emit waves that affect the brain, causing these effects:

- Frustration and/or rage.
- Superstitious beliefs ("the computer hates me") and magical thinking ("the programme only works when I wear my hat backward").
- Random-walk programming (the attempt to

programme by writing every possible programme and choosing the one that does the right thing).

If you find yourself suffering from any of these symptoms, get up and go for a walk. When you are calm, think about the programme. What is it doing? What are some possible causes of that behaviour? When was the last time you had a working programme, and what did you do next?

Sometimes it just takes time to find a bug. We often find bugs when we are away from the computer and let our minds wander. Some of the best places to find bugs are trains, showers, and in bed, just before you fall asleep.

No, I really need help.

It happens. Even the best programmers occasionally get stuck. Sometimes you work on a programme so long that you can't see the error. A fresh pair of eyes is just the thing.

Before you bring someone else in, make sure you have exhausted the techniques described here. Your programme should be as simple as possible, and you should be working on the smallest input that causes the error.

You should have printstatements in the appropriate places (and the output they produce should be comprehensible). You should understand the problem well enough to describe it concisely.

When you bring someone in to help, be sure to give them the information they need:

- If there is an error message, what is it and what part of the programme does it indicate?
- What was the last thing you did before this error occurred? What were the last lines of code that you wrote, or what is the new test case that fails?
- What have you tried so far, and what have you learned?

When you find the bug, take a second to think about what you could have done to find it faster. Next time you see something similar, you will be able to find the bug more quickly.

Remember, the goal is not just to make the programme work. The goal is to learn how to make the programme work.

CREATING A NEW DATA TYPE

Object-oriented programming languages allow programmers to create new data types that behave much like built-in data types. We will explore this capability by building a Fraction class that works very much like the built-in numeric types: integers, longs and floats.

Fractions, also known as rational numbers, are values that can be expressed as a ratio of whole numbers, such as **5/6**. The top number is called the numerator and the bottom number is called the denominator.

We start by defining a **Fraction** *class with an initialization method that provides the numerator and denominator as integers*:

```
class Fraction:
def __init__(self, numerator,
denominator=1):
self.numerator = numerator
self.denominator = denominator
```

The denominator is optional. A Fraction with just one parameter represents a whole number. If the numerator is **n**, we build the Fraction **n/1**.

The next step is to write a **__str__** method that displays fractions in a way that makes sense. The form "numerator/denominator" is natural here:

```
class Fraction:
...
def __str__(self):
    return "%d/%d"% (self.numerator,
            self.denominator)
```

To test what we have so far, we put it in a file named **Fraction.py** and import it into the Python interpreter. Then we create a fraction object and print it.

```
from Fraction import Fraction
spam = Fraction(5,6)
print "The fraction is", spam
The fraction is 5/6
```

As usual, the print command invokes the **__str__** method implicitly.

FRACTION MULTIPLICATION

We would like to be able to apply the normal addition, subtraction, multiplication, and division operations to fractions. To do this, we can overload the mathematical operators for **Fraction** objects.

We'll start with multiplication because it is the easiest to implement. To multiply fractions, we create a new fraction with a numerator that is the product of the original numerators and a denominator that is a product of the original denominators. **__mul__** is the name Python uses for a method that overloads the *operator:

```
class Fraction:
    ...
    def __mul__(self, other):
        return Fraction (self. numerator *
other                  .numerator,

self.denominator* other.
                 denominator)
```

We can test this method by computing the product of two fractions:

```
print Fraction(5,6) * Fraction(3,4)
15/24
```

It works, but we can do better! We can extend the method to handle multiplication by an integer.

We use the **isinstance** *function to test if* **other** is an integer and convert it to a fraction if it is.

```
class Fraction:
    ...
    def __mul__(self, other):
        if isinstance(other, int):
            other = Fraction(other)
        return Fraction(self.numerator *
other.
                      numerator,
    self.denominator * other.
                          denominator)
```

Multiplying fractions and integers now works, but only if the fraction is the left operand:

```
print Fraction(5,6) * 4
20/6
print 4 * Fraction(5,6)
TypeError: __mul__ nor __rmul__ defined for
    these operands
```

To evaluate a binary operator like multiplication, Python checks the left operand first to see if it provides a **__mul__** that supports the type of the second operand. In this case, the built-in integer operator doesn't support fractions.

Next, Python checks the right operand to see if it provides an **__rmul__** method that supports the first type. In this case, we haven't provided **__rmul__**, so it fails.

On the other hand, there is a simple way to provide **__rmul__**:

```
class Fraction:
...
__rmul__ = __mul__
```

This assignment says that the **__rmul__** is the same as **__mul__**. Now if we evaluate **4 * Fraction(5,6)**, Python invokes **__rmul__** on the **Fraction** object and passes 4 as a parameter:

```
print 4 * Fraction(5,6)
20/6
```

Since **__rmul__** is the same as **__mul__**, and **__mul__** can handle an integer parameter, we're all set.

FRACTION ADDITION

Addition is more complicated than multiplication, but still not too bad. The sum ofa/b and c/d is the fraction **(a*d+c*b)/(b*d)**.

Using the multiplication code as a model, we can write **__add__** and **__radd__**:

```
class Fraction:
    ...
    def __add__(self, other):
        if isinstance(other, int):
            other = Fraction(other)
        return Fraction(self.numerator *
```

```
                                other.  denominator +
                        self.denominator * other.
                                numerator,
                            self.denominator * other.
                            denominator)
    __radd__ = __add__
```

We can test these methods with Fractions and integers.

```
print Fraction(5,6) + Fraction(5,6)
60/36
print Fraction(5,6) + 3
23/6
print 2 + Fraction(5,6)
17/6
```

The first two examples invoke **__add__**; the last invokes **__radd__**.

Euclid's algorithm

In the previous example, we computed the sum 5/6 + 5/6 and got 60/36. That is correct, but it's not the best way to represent the answer. To reduce the fraction to its simplest terms, we have to divide the numerator and denominator by their greatest common divisor (GCD), which is 12. The result is 5/3.

In general, whenever we create a new Fraction object, we should reduce it by dividing the numerator and denominator by their GCD. If the fraction is already reduced, the GCD is 1.

Euclid of Alexandria (approx. 325—265 BCE) presented an algorithm to find the GCD for two integers m and n:

If n divides m evenly, then n is the GCD. Otherwise the GCD is the GCD of n and the remainder of m divided by n.

This recursive definition can be expressed concisely as a function:

```
def gcd (m, n):
    if m% n == 0:
        return n
else:
        return gcd(n, m%n)
```

In the first line of the body, we use the modulus operator to check divisibility. On the last line, we use it to compute the remainder after division. Since all the operations we've written create new **Fractions** for the result, we can reduce all results by modifying the initialization method.

```
    class Fraction:
        def    __init__(self,   numerator,
denominator=1):
            g = gcd (numerator, denominator)
            self.numerator = numerator / g
            self.denominator = denominator / g
```

Now whenever we create a **Fraction**, it is reduced to its simplest form:

```
    Fraction(100,-36)
    -25/9
```

A nice feature of **gcd** is that if the fraction is negative, the minus sign is always moved to the numerator.

COMPARING FRACTIONS

Suppose we have two **Fraction** objects, **a** and **b**, and we evaluate **a == b**. The default implementation of **==** tests for shallow equality, so it only returns true if **a**and **b** are the same object.

By convention, the **__cmp__** method returns a negative number if **self** is less than**other**, zero if they are the same, and a positive number if **self** is greater than **other**.

The simplest way to compare fractions is to cross-multiply. If **a/b > c/d**, then**ad > bc**. With that in mind, here is the code for **__cmp__**:

```
    class Fraction:
    ...
def __cmp__(self, other):
        diff    =     (self.numerator     *
other.denominator                -
                    other.numerator     *
self.denominator)
                    return diff
```

If **self** is greater than **other**, then **diff** will be positive. If **other** is greater, then **diff**will be negative. If they are the same, **diff** is zero.

TAKING IT FURTHER

Of course, we are not done. We still have to implement subtraction by overriding**__sub__** and division by overriding **__div__**.

One way to handle those operations is to implement negation by overriding **__neg__**and inversion by overriding **__invert__**. Then we can subtract by negating the second operand and adding, and we can divide by inverting the second operand and multiplying.

Next, we have to provide **__rsub__** and **__rdiv__**. Unfortunately, we can't use the same trick we used for addition and multiplication, because subtraction and division are not commutative. We can't just set __rsub__ and __rdiv__ equal to**__sub__** and **__div__**. In these operations, the order of the operands makes a difference.

To handle unary negation, which is the use of the minus sign with a single operand, we override **__neg__**.

We can compute powers by overriding **__pow__**, but the implementation is a little tricky. If the exponent isn't an integer, then it may not be possible to represent the result as a **Fraction**. For example, **Fraction(2) Fraction(1,2)** is the square root of 2, which is an irrational number (it can't be represented as a fraction). So it's not easy to write the most general version of **__pow__**.

There is one other extension to the **Fraction** class that you might want to think about. So far, we have assumed that the numerator and denominator are integers.

The translated programme is in machine language and often called as a.out. But it can have any name. Before the compiler creates a machine language programme, it creates an intermediate file which has an ending.o.

This file is called the object code. So, let us assume that you have made a programme called *foo.f* On compilation, an object file *foo.o* and an executable a.out is created by the computer. Other possible names of the compiler are fort, g77, f90, lf90 (only in the Institute of Physics and on some of the machines) etc. The output of the command is foo.o and a.out. To run the programme, type

```
a.out
  or
./a.out
```

at the command prompt. The programme will then be executed.

The steps involved in computing using fortran:

- Make a programme file (eg *foo.f*) using any editor of your choice
- Compile the file and make an object code (*foo.o*) and an executable file (usually *a.out*)
- Execute the programme (*a.out*)
- Check the results for errors, correct the errors in the fortran programme and go back to step 2

The Fortran compiler, by default, creates executable file named a.out after compilation. The problem with default is every compiled file is a.out so one doesn't know what it does if you have a number of programmes.

Also, every time you compile a new programme, old a.out is erased and new a.out is written in it's place. So, it is convinient to follow a convention where the executable of a Fortran programme has a name similar to the name of the fortran programme. The convention I follow is to name the executable as foo. The command to generate this executable is

f77 -o foo foo.f

It appears that the object file foo.o is of no use. As mentioned above, the object file is a programme which is between a fortran programme and its executable code. It is useful when one has a number of subunits (subroutines, functions, libraries) in a fortran programme and if one is modifying only a part of a programme, it doesn't make sense to compile all the other programme units again and again. In this case, one can compile the programme that is changed and use link the object code thus created with the object codes of other programme units.

This saves a lot of compilation time, particularly if one has tens of other programme units. During the course of these lectures we will not be dealing with complicated and lengthy programmes and as a result we will not be using the object files in the course.

XML LANGUAGE

C is a relatively small language, but one which wears well. C's small, unambitious feature set is a real advantage: there's less to learn; there isn't excess baggage in the way when you don't need it. It can also be a disadvantage: since it doesn't do everything for you, there's a lot you have to do yourself.

C is sometimes referred to as a "high-level assembly language." Some people think that's an insult, but it's actually a deliberate and significant aspect of the language. If you have programmed in assembly language, you'll probably find C very natural and comfortable (although if you continue to focus too heavily on machine-level details, you'll probably end up with unnecessarily nonportable programmes). If you haven't programmed in assembly language, you may be frustrated by C's lack of certain higher-level features.

In either case, you should understand why C was designed this way: so that seemingly-simple constructions expressed in C would not expand to arbitrarily expensive (in time or space) machine language constructions when compiled. If you write a C programme simply and succinctly, it is likely to result in a succinct, efficient machine language executable. If you find that the executable programme resulting from a C programme is not efficient, it's probably because of something silly you did, not because of something the compiler did behind your back which you have no control over. In any case, there's no point in complaining about C's low-level flavour: C is what it is.

A programming language is a tool, and no tool can perform every task unaided. If you're building a house, and I'm teaching you how to use a hammer, and you ask how to assemble rafters and trusses into gables, that's a legitimate question, but the answer has fallen out of the realm of "How do I use a hammer?" and into "How do I build a house?". In the same way, we'll see that C does not have built-in features to perform every function that we might ever need to do while programming.

As mentioned above, C imposes relatively few built-in ways of doing things on the programmer. Some common tasks, such as manipulating strings, allocating memory, and doing input/output (I/O), are performed by calling on library functions. Other tasks which you might want to do, such as creating or listing directories, or interacting with a mouse, or displaying windows or other user-interface elements, or doing colour graphics, are not defined by the C language at all. You can do these things from a C programme, of course, but you will be calling on services which are peculiar to your programming environment (compiler, processor, and operating system) and which are not defined by the C standard. Since this course is about portable C programming, it will also be steering clear of facilities not provided in all C environments.

Another aspect of C that's worth mentioning here is that it is, to put it bluntly, a bit dangerous. C does not, in general, try hard to protect a programmer from mistakes. If you write a piece of code which will (through some oversight of yours) do something wildly different from what you intended it to do, up to and including deleting your data or trashing your disk, and if it is possible for the compiler to compile it, it generally will. You won't get warnings of the form "Do you really mean to...?" or "Are you sure you really want to...?". C is often compared to a sharp knife: it can do a surgically precise job on some exacting task you have in mind, but it can also do a surgically precise job of cutting off your finger. It's up to you to use it carefully.

This aspect of C is very widely criticized; it is also used (justifiably) to argue that C is not a good teaching language. C aficionados love this aspect of C because it means that C does not try to protect them from themselves: when they know what they're doing, even if it's risky or obscure, they can do it. Students of C hate this aspect of C because it often seems as if the language is some kind of a conspiracy specifically designed to lead them into booby traps.

This is another aspect of the language which it's fairly pointless to complain about. If you take care and pay attention, you can avoid many of the pitfalls. These notes will point out many of the obvious (and not so obvious) trouble spots.

EXAMPLE

The best way to learn programming is to dive right in and start writing real programmes. This way, concepts which would otherwise seem abstract make sense, and the positive feedback you get from getting even a small programme to work gives you a great incentive to improve it or write the next one.

Diving in with "real" programmes right away has another advantage, if only pragmatic: if you're using a conventional compiler, you can't run a fragment of a programme and see what it does; nothing will run until you have a complete (if tiny or trivial) programme. You can't learn everything you'd need to write a complete programme all at once, so you'll have to take some things "on faith" and parrot them in your first programmes before you begin to understand them. (You can't learn to programme just one expression or statement at a time any more than you can learn to speak a foreign language one word at a time. If all you know is a handful of words, you can't actually *say* anything: you also need to know something about the language's word order and grammar and sentence structure and declension of articles and verbs.)

Besides the occasional necessity to take things on faith, there is a more serious potential drawback of this "dive in and programme" approach: it's a small step from learning-by-doing to learning-by-trial-and-error, and when you learn programming by trial-and-error, you can very easily learn many errors. When you're not sure whether something will work, or you're not even sure what you could use that might work, and you try something, and it does work, you do *not* have any guarantee that what you tried worked for the right reason. You might just have "learned" something that works only by accident or only on your compiler, and it may be very hard to un-learn it later, when it stops working.

Therefore, whenever you're not sure of something, be very careful before you go off and try it "just to see if it will work." Of course, you can never be absolutely sure that something is going to work before you try it, otherwise we'd never have to try things.

But you should have an expectation that something is going to work before you try it, and if you can't predict how to do something or whether something would work and find yourself having to determine it experimentally, make a note in your mind that whatever you've just learned (based on the outcome of the experiment) is suspect.

The first example programme is the first example programme in any language: print or display a simple string, and exit. Here is "hello, world" programme:

```
#include <stdio.h>
main()
{
printf("Hello, world!\n");
return 0;
}
```

If you have a C compiler, the first thing to do is figure out how to type this programme in and compile it and run it and see where its output went.The first line is practically boilerplate; it will appear in almost all programmes we write. It asks that some definitions having to do with the "Standard I/O Library" be included in our programme; these definitions are needed if we are to call the library function printf correctly.

The second line says that we are defining a function named main. Most of the time, we can name our functions anything we want, but the function name main is special: it is the function that will be "called" first when our programme starts running. The empty pair of parentheses indicates that our main function accepts no*arguments,* that is, there isn't any information which needs to be passed in when the function is called.

The braces { and } surround a list of statements in C. Here, they surround the list of statements making up the function main.

The line

```
printf("Hello, world!\n");
```

is the first statement in the programme. It asks that the function printf be called; printf is a library function which prints formatted output. The parentheses surroundprintf's argument list: the information which is handed to it which it should act on. The semicolon at the end of the line terminates the statement.

(printf's name reflects the fact that C was first developed when Teletypes and other printing terminals were still in widespread use. Today, of course, video displays are far more common. printf's "prints" to the *standard output,* that is, to the default location for programme output to go. Nowadays, that's almost always a video screen or a window on that screen. If you do have a printer, you'll typically have to do something extra to get a programme to print to it.)

printf's first (and, in this case, only) argument is the string which it should print. The string, enclosed in double quotes "", consists of the words "Hello, world!" followed by a special sequence: \n. In strings, any two-character sequence beginning with the backslash \ represents a single special character. The sequence \nrepresents the "new line" character, which prints a carriage return or line feed or whatever it takes to end one line of output and move down to the next. (This programme only prints one line of output, but it's still important to terminate it.)

The second line in the main function is:

```
return 0;
```

In general, a function may return a value to its caller, and main is no exception. When main returns (that is, reaches its end and stops functioning), the programme is at its end, and the return value from main tells the operating system (or whatever invoked the programme that main is the main function of) whether it succeeded or not. By convention, a return value of 0 indicates success.

This programme may look so absolutely trivial that it seems as if it's not even worth typing it in and trying to run it, but doing so may be a big (and is certainly a vital) first hurdle.

On an unfamiliar computer, it can be arbitrarily difficult to figure out how to enter a text file containing programme source, or how to compile and link it, or how to invoke it, or what happened after (if?) it ran.

The most experienced C programmers immediately go back to this one, simple programme whenever they're trying out a new system or a new way of entering or building programmes or a new way of printing output from within programmes. As Kernighan and Ritchie say, everything else is comparatively easy.

How *you* compile and run this (or any) programme is a function of the compiler and operating system you're using. The first step is to type it in, exactly as shown; this may involve using a text editor to create a file containing the programme text. You'll have to give the file a name, and all C compilers require that files containing C source end with the extension .c. So you might place the programme text in a file called hello.c.

The second step is to compile the programme. (Strictly speaking, compilation consists of two steps, compilation proper followed by linking, but we can overlook this distinction at first, especially because the compiler often takes care of initiating the linking step automatically.) On many Unix systems, the command to compile a C programme from a source file hello.c is

```
cc -o hello hello.c
```

You would type this command at the Unix shell prompt, and it requests that the cc (C compiler) programme be run, placing its output (i.e. the new executable programme it creates) in the file hello, and taking its input (i.e. the source code to be compiled) from the file hello.c.

The third step is to run (execute, invoke) the newly-built hello programme. Again on a Unix system, this is done simply by typing the program's name:

hello

Depending on how your system is set up (in particular, on whether the current directory is searched for executables, based on the PATH variable), you may have to type ./hello to indicate that the hello programme is in the current directory (as opposed to some "bin" directory full of executable programmes, elsewhere).

You may also have your choice of C compilers. On many Unix machines, the cc command is an older compiler which does not recognize modern, ANSI Standard C syntax. An old compiler will accept the simple programmes we'll be starting with, but it will not accept most of our later programmes. If you find yourself getting baffling compilation errors on programmes which you've typed in exactly as they're shown, it probably indicates that you're using an older compiler. On many machines, another compiler called acc or gcc is available, and you'll want to use it, instead. (Both acc and gcc are typically invoked the same as cc; that is, the above cc command would instead be typed, say, gcc -o hello hello.c .)

(One final caveat about Unix systems: don't name your test programmes test, because there's already a standard command called test, and you and the command interpreter will get badly confused if you try to replace the system's test command with your own, not least because your own almost certainly does something completely different.)

Under MS-DOS, the compilation procedure is quite similar. The name of the command you type will depend on your compiler (e.g. cl for the Microsoft C compiler,tc or bcc for Borland's Turbo C, etc.). You may have to manually perform the second, linking step, perhaps with a command named link or tlink. The executable file which the compiler/ linker creates will have a name ending in .exe (or perhaps .com), but you can still invoke it by typing the base name (*e.g.* hello). See your compiler documentation for complete details; one of the manuals should contain a demonstration of how to enter, compile, and run a small programme that prints some simple output, just as we're trying to describe here.

In an integrated or "visual" progamming environment, such as those on the Macintosh or under various versions of Microsoft Windows, the steps you take to enter, compile, and run a programme are somewhat different (and, theoretically, simpler). Typically, there is a way to open a new source window, type source code into it, give it a file name, and add it to the programme (or "project") you're building. If necessary, there will be a way to specify what other source files (or "modules") make up the programme. Then, there's a button or menu selection which compiles and runs the programme, all from within the programming environment.

(There will also be a way to create a standalone executable file which you can run from outside the environment.) In a PC-compatible environment, you may have to choose between creating DOS programmes or Windows programmes. (If you have troubles pertaining to the printf function, try specifying a target environment of MS-DOS.

Supposedly, some compilers which are targeted at Windows environments won't let you call printf, because until you call some fancier functions to request that a window be created, there's no window for printf to print to.) Again, check the introductory or tutorial manual that came with the programming package; it should walk you through the steps necessary to get your first programme running.

PROGRAMME STRUCTURE

We'll have more to say later about programme structure, but for now let's observe a few basics. A programme consists of one or more functions; it may also contain global variables. (Our two example programmes so far have contained one function apiece, and no global variables.) At the top of a source file are typically a few boilerplate lines such as #include <stdio.h>, followed by the definitions (i.e. code) for the functions.

Each function is further composed of *declarations* and *statements*, in that order. When a sequence of statements should act as one (for example, when they should all serve together as the body of a loop) they can be enclosed in braces (just as for the outer body of the entire function). The simplest kind of statement is an *expression statement*, which is an expression (presumably performing some useful operation) followed by a semicolon. Expressions are further composed of *operators*, *objects*(variables), and *constants*.

C source code consists of several *lexical elements*. Some are words, such as for, return, main, and i, which are either *keywords* of the language (for, return) or *identifiers* (names) we've chosen for our own functions and variables (main, i). There are *constants* such as 1 and 10 which introduce new values into the programme.

There are *operators* such as =, +, and >, which manipulate variables and values. There are other punctuation characters (often called *delimiters*), such as parentheses and squiggly braces {}, which indicate how the other elements of the programme are grouped. Finally, all of the preceding elements can be separated by*whitespace*: spaces, tabs, and the "carriage returns" between lines.

The source code for a C programme is, for the most part, "free form." This means that the compiler does not care how the code is arranged: how it is broken into lines, how the lines are indented, or whether whitespace is used between things like variable names and other punctuation. (Lines like #include <stdio.h> are an exception; they must appear alone on their own lines, generally unbroken.

Only lines beginning with # are affected by this rule; we'll see other examples later.) You can use whitespace, indentation, and appropriate line breaks to make your programmes more readable for yourself and other people (even though the compiler doesn't care). You can place explanatory *comments* anywhere in your programme—any text between the characters /* and */ is ignored by the compiler. (In fact, the compiler pretends that all it saw was whitespace.) Though comments are ignored by the compiler, well-chosen comments can make a programme *much* easier to read.

The usage of whitespace is our first *style* issue. It's typical to leave a blank line between different parts of the programme, to leave a space on either side of operators such as + and =, and to *indent* the bodies of loops and other control flow constructs.

Typically, we arrange the indentation so that the subsidiary statements controlled by a loop statement (the "loop body," such as the printf call in our second example programme) are all aligned with each other and placed one tab stop (or some consistent number of spaces) to the right of the controlling statement.

This indentation (like all whitespace) is not required by the compiler, but it makes programs*much* easier to read. (However, it can also be misleading, if used incorrectly or in the face of inadvertent mistakes.

The compiler will decide what "the body of the loop" is based on its own rules, not the indentation, so if the indentation does not match the compiler's interpretation, confusion is inevitable.)

To drive home the point that the compiler doesn't care about indentation, line breaks, or other whitespace, here are a few (extreme) examples: The fragments

```
for(i = 0; i < 10; i = i + 1)
printf("%d\n", i);
```

and

```
for(i = 0; i < 10; i = i + 1) printf("%d\n",
i);
```

and

```
for(i=0;i<10;i=i+1)printf("%d\n",i);
```

and

```
for(i = 0; i < 10; i = i + 1)
printf("%d\n", i);
```

and

```
    for    (    i
    =      0    ;
    i      <    10
    ;      i    =
    i      +    1
    )  printf  (
  "%d\n"   ,    i
    )        ;
```

and

```
  for
 (i=0;
 i<10;i=
 i+1)printf
```

```
("%d\n", i);
```

are all treated exactly the same way by the compiler.

Some programmers argue forever over the best set of "rules" for indentation and other aspects of programming style, calling to mind the old philosopher's debates about the number of angels that could dance on the head of a pin. Style issues (such as how a programme is laid out) *are* important, but they're not something to be too dogmatic about, and there are also other, deeper style issues besides mere layout and typography:

Although C compilers do not care about how a programme looks, proper indentation and spacing are critical in making programmes easy for people to read. We recommend writing only one statement per line, and using blanks around operators to clarify grouping. The position of braces is less important, although people hold passionate beliefs. We have chosen one of several popular styles. Pick a style that suits you, then use it consistently.

There is some value in having a reasonably standard style (or a few standard styles) for code layout. Please don't take the above advice to "pick a style that suits you" as an invitation to invent your own brand-new style. If (perhaps after you've been programming in C for a while) you have specific objections to specific facets of existing styles, you're welcome to modify them, but if you don't have any particular leanings, you're probably best off copying an existing style at first. (If you want to place your own stamp of originality on the programmes that you write, there are better avenues for your creativity than inventing a bizarre layout; you might instead try to make the logic easier to follow, or the user interface easier to use, or the code freer of bugs.).

VARIABLES

A variable is a symbolic name for a memory location in which data can be stored and subsequently recalled. Variables are used for holding data values so that they can be utilized in various computations in a programme. The value of variable can change during the exectution of programme.

All variables have two important attributes:

1. A type which is established when the variable is defined (e.g., integer, real, character). Once defined, the type of a C++ variable cannot be changed.
2. A value which can be changed by assigning a new value to the variable. The kind of values a variable can assume depends on its type. For example, an integer variable can only take integer values (e.g., 2, 100, -12). Listing 1.2 illustrates the uses of some simple variable.

```
1 # include <iostream.h>
2 int main (void)
3 {
4  int workDays;
5  float workHours, payRate, weeklyPay;
6  workDays = 5;
7  workHours = 7.5;
8  payRate = 38.55;
9  weeklyPay = workDays * workHours * payRate;
10  cout << "Weekly Pay = ";
11  cout << weeklyPay;
12  cout << '\n';
13 }
```

ANNOTATION

4. This line defines an int (integer) variable called workDays, which will represent the number of working days in a week. As a general rule, a variable is defined by specifying its type first, followed by the variable name, followed by a semicolon.
5. This line defines three float (real) variables which, respectively, represent the work hours per day, the hourly pay rate, and the weekly pay. As illustrated by this line, multiple variables of the same type can be defined at once by separating them with commas.
6. This line is an assignment statement. It assigns the

value 5 to the variable workDays. Therefore, after this statement is executed, workDays denotes the value 5.

7. This line assigns the value 7.5 to the variable workHours.
8. This line assigns the value 38.55 to the variable payRate.
9. This line calculates the weekly pay as the product of workDays, workHours, and payRate (* is the multiplication operator). The resulting value is stored in weeklyPay.

10-12. These lines output three items in sequence: the string "Weekly Pay = ", the value of the variable weeklyPay, and a newline character. When run, the programme will produce the following output:

```
Weekly Pay = 1445.625
```

When a variable is defined, its value is undefined until it is actually assigned one. For example, weeklyPay has an undefined value/unpredictable value (i.e., whatever happens to be in the memory location which the variable denotes at the time) until line 9 is executed.

INITIALIZATION

It is important to ensure that a variable is initialized before it is used in any computation. It is possible to define a variable and initialize it at the same time. This is considered a good programming practice, because it pre-empts the possibility of using the variable prior to it being initialized. For all intents and purposes, the two programmes are equivalent.

```
#include <iostream.h>
int main (void)
{
 int workDays = 5;
 float workHours = 7.5;
 float payRate = 38.55;
 float weeklyPay = workDays * workHours * payRate;
 cout << "Weekly Pay = ";
```

```
cout << weeklyPay;
 cout << '\n';
}
```

SIMPLE INPUT/OUTPUT

The most common way in which a programme communicates with the outside world is through simple, character-oriented Input/Output (IO) operations. C++ provides two useful operators for this purpose: >> for input and << for output. We have already seen examples of output using <<. Listing below illustrates the use of >> for input.

```
1 #include <iostream.h>
2 int main (void)
3 {
4  int workDays = 5;
5  float workHours = 7.5;
6  float payRate, weeklyPay;
7  cout << "What is the hourly pay rate? ";
8  cin >> payRate;
9  weeklyPay = workDays * workHours * payRate;
10  cout << "Weekly Pay = ";
11  cout << weeklyPay;
12  cout << '\n';
13 }
```

ANNOTATION

7. This line outputs the prompt What is the hourly pay rate? to seek user input.
8. This line reads the input value typed by the user and copies it to payRate. The input operator >> takes an input stream as its left operand (cin is the standard C++ input stream which corresponds to data entered via the keyboard) and a variable (to which the input data is copied) as its right operand.

9-13. The rest of the programme is as before. When run, the programme will produce the following output (user input appears in bold):

```
What is the hourly pay rate? 33.55
Weekly Pay = 1258.125
```

Both << and >> return their left operand as their result, enabling multiple input or multiple output operations to be combined into one statement. This is illustrated by Listing below which now allows the input of both the daily work hours and the hourly pay rate.

```
1 #include <iostream.h>
2 int main (void)
3 {
4  int workDays = 5;
5  float workHours, payRate, weeklyPay;
6  cout << "What are the work hours and the hourly pay rate? ";
7  cin >> workHours >> payRate;
8  weeklyPay = workDays * workHours * payRate;
9  cout << "Weekly Pay = " << weeklyPay << '\n';
10 }
```

ANNOTATION

7 This line reads two input values typed by the user and copies them to workHours and payRate, respectively. The two values should be separated by white space (*i.e.*, one or more space or tab characters). This statement is equivalent to:

```
(cin >> workHours) >> payRate;
```

Because the result of >> is its left operand, (cin >> workHours) evaluates to cin which is then used as the left operand of the next >> operator.

9 This line is the result of combining lines 10-12 from Listing 1.4. It outputs "Weekly Pay = ", followed by the value of weeklyPay, followed by a newline character. This statement is equivalent to:

```
((cout << "Weekly Pay = ") << weeklyPay)
    << '\n';
```

Because the result of << is its left operand, (cout << "Weekly Pay = ") evaluates to cout which is then used as the left operand of the next << operator, etc.

When run, the programme will produce the following output:

```
What are the work hours and the hourly pay rate? 7.5 33.55
Weekly Pay = 1258.125.
```

COMMENTS

A comment is a piece of descriptive text which explains some aspect of a programme. Programme comments are totally ignored by the compiler and are only intended for human readers. C++ provides two types of comment delimiters:

- Anything after//(until the end of the line on which it appears) is considered a comment.
- Anything enclosed by the pair/* and */is considered a comment.

Listing 1.6 illustrates the use of both forms.

Listing 1.6

```
#include <iostream.h>
/* This programme calculates the weekly gross pay for a worker,
based on the total number of hours worked and the hourly pay
rate. */
int main (void)
{
int workDays = 5;    // Number of work days per week
float workHours = 7.5;    // Number of work hours per day
float payRate = 33.50;    // Hourly pay rate
float weeklyPay;    // Gross weekly pay
weeklyPay = workDays * workHours * payRate;
cout << "Weekly Pay = " << weeklyPay << '\n';
}
```

Comments should be used to enhance (not to hinder) the readability of a programme.

Bibliography

Beverly V.: *FileMaker Pro 6 Developer's Guide to XML/XSL*, London: Longman Publication, 2003.

Bill E.: *Professional VB.NET 2003*, London: Bski International Press, 2004.

Christian N.: *Professional C# 2006*, New Work: Microsoft Office Press, 2006.

Gary B. S.: *Comprehensive Concepts and Techniques*, New York: Chapman and Hall, 2001.

Ian F.D.: *Java Cookbook*, New York: Addison-Wesley Press, 2003.

Julitta K.: *Excel 2003 Vba Programming With XML And ASP*, London: Oxford University Press, 2000.

Kent S.: *Professional XML*, New York: Cambridge University Press, 2006.

Kirstan V.: *XML-Based Integration with XAware: Unifying Applications and Data*, New York: Cambridge University Press, 2001.

Larry L.: *Hack Proofing XML*, New York: National Biomedical Research Foundation, 2004.

Lucinda D.: *Dynamic Web Application Development Using XML and Java*, New York: Journal of Experimental Botany, 2003.

Lucinda, D.: *XML for Dummies*, London: Academic Press, 2002.

Mcfarlane: *Definitive XSL-FO*, London: Longman Publication, 2003.

Michael F.: *Special edition using XSLT*, London: Methuen Press, 2000.

Michael M.: *Sams Teach Yourself XML in 24 Hours*, New York: Wiley Press, 2001.

Patrick C.: *Core Web Programming*, New York: O'Reilly Media, 2003.

Powell: *Beginning XML Databases* , Paris: Masson et Cie Press, 2005.

Mangano : *XSLT Cookbook*, New York: Columbia University Press, 2002.

Sharon D.: *XML Made Simple*, Eugene: Oregon State University Press, 2005.

Shaun W.: *Professional Dotnetnuke*, Austin: Rinehart and Winston Publication, 2003.

Tidwell: *XSLT*, Cambridge: Massachusetts Publication, 2004.

Williamson: *XML: The Complete Reference*, New York: Addison-Wesley Press, 2003.

Zarella L.R.: *XSLT and XPath: a Guide to XML Transormations*, New York: Addison-Wesley Press, 2001.

Index